LEADERS FOR GOD'S NATION

GREAT WORSHIP FOR KIDS

Middler/Junior

STANDARD PUBLISHING
Cincinnati, Ohio

Session Writers

Kathleen Underwood, Sessions 1-4
Vicki Ziese, Sessions 5-9
Diana Crawford, Sessions 10-13

Activity Pages

Richard Bills
Dawn Korth
Dina Sorn
Michael Streff

Scripture quotations marked *NIV* are from the HOLY BIBLE—NEW INTERNATIONAL VERSION, Copyright © 1973, 1978, 1984 International Bible Society. Used by permission of Zondervan Bible Publishers.

Scriptures marked *ICB* quoted from the *International Children's Bible, New Century Version,* copyright © 1986, 1988 by Word Publishing, Dallas, Texas 75039. Used by permission.

The Standard Publishing Company, Cincinnati, Ohio
A division of Standex International Corporation
©1994 by The Standard Publishing Company

All rights reserved.
Printed in the United States of America

ISBN 0-7847-0015-X

Table of Contents

Unit One: Leaders Believe God's Promises

1. God Promises to Be With Us — 9
   Promises, Promises, 13 • On the Air, 14 • Crossword Review, 15
2. God Promises to Protect Us — 16
   Pen a Praise Poem, 20 • Write a Prayer, 21 • Secret Code, 22
3. God's Word Promises Guidance — 23
   Prayer Journal, 27 • Believe It! 28
4. God Promises to Answer Our Prayers — 29
   Praise Acrostic, 33 • Does God Listen? 34 • Mystery Reminder, 35

Unit Two: Leaders Trust God

5. Jesus Is Alive! — 36
   Write an Interview, 40 • Joy or Sorrow? 41 • Worship Cube, 42
6. With God, Nothing Is Impossible — 43
   Praise God! 47 • Make a Puzzle, 48 • Make a "God Helps Me" Book, 49
7. The World's Strongest Man Becomes Weak — 50
   Find the Strength, 54 • The Strength God Gave, 55
8. God Speaks: We Listen — 56
   Finish the Story, 60 • Look for Truth, 61 • Schedule Your Scripture Reading, 62
9. Be Good Followers — 63
   Put Them in Order! 67 • Follow the Leader, 68 • Choose to Follow, 69

Unit Three: Leaders Please God

10. An Obedient Heart — 70
    One of a Kind, 74 • God's View of You, 75 • Heart Surgery, 76
11. A Loving Heart — 77
    Friendtalk, 81 • To the Rescue! 82 • Make a Mobile, 83
12. A Wise Heart — 84
    Wisdom Watcher, 88 • Proverbs Mix-Up, 89
13. A Respectful Heart — 90
    Heartfelt Gratitude, 94 • News Broadcast Skit, 95 • God Answers Prayer/God Keeps His Promises, 96

Introduction

It Doesn't Seem Great to Me . . .

What do you mean?

Great worship . . . Our Middler/Junior worship is hardly what you'd call great.

Why is that?

Well, I guess everyone has a different idea of what our worship time should be. Our Bible school superintendent calls it "extended session," and wants us to have a second Sunday school hour. But Sunday school is designed for instruction. Our worship time is for worshiping God.

That makes sense to me. What do the parents think?

Some of them want us to have a carbon copy of an adult worship service—including a sermon.

Uh-oh. That's not realistic for many Middlers and Juniors, is it?

In my experience it's not. Kids that age don't think like adults, respond like adults—and they certainly don't sit still as long as adults! I want them to worship God in ways that are appropriate for their level of development.

Absolutely. And you're not just keeping them occupied while their parents are in worship, as some people believe. The children's worship is as important and meaningful as the parents'.

Yes. I want every kid there to know God personally and to respond to Him in praise and thanksgiving. I want the kids to learn that worship is active, not passive. It's something they themselves do—not just the leader in front of the group.

Sounds to me as if you're right on target. What makes your Middler/Junior worship less than great?

It's hard to involve all the pupils sometimes. There are older kids and younger kids. Some are quick and bright, and some work more slowly and need more encouragement. Some are more comfortable in small groups than others. It's hard to appeal to all their differences.

The writers of *Great Worship for Kids* know that's true. They've tried to consider individual differences as they've planned worship sessions. As you examine each session you'll find some activities that are easy, some that are more difficult. Some appeal to pupils who like to research or to work puzzles, and some to pupils who like to speak and act. Each session will have something that addresses the needs of each pupil.

I guess so. And even if a pupil doesn't get into the activities one week, the following week he can find something he likes. But while we're talking about the number of activities in each session, what about the number of adult leaders needed for all the small groups? There are only two of us, and we can't be everywhere!

One solution is to use a cassette recorder. Tape record instructions for one or more of the small groups and have those groups work independently. Or photocopy the instructions for pupils to read. Ask an older or more mature pupil to serve as "chairperson" of the group to keep things moving.

I've tried that. As a matter of fact, during the week before the session I contact pupils to be chairpersons. That way I can give them special instructions so they'll be prepared. And it's good to get to know the pupils better and make them feel special.

Great! And then during *Building the Theme* you can circulate between groups as they need attention. You can also choose only one or two activities to prepare in small groups, and do the rest of the session as a large group. And—though it's not ideal—you can always omit parts of *Sharing in Worship* if they can't be prepared in small groups.

I always hate to leave things out. But actually, I feel as though we get into a rut sometimes anyway, so I guess it's not so bad to drop something from time to time. We do many of the same things every week. Take music, for instance. The kids either write words for a song, sing songs, or choose songs for the group to sing. It's so predictable!

So is adult worship. Think about what is done in most churches today—the same things, often in the same order, Sunday after Sunday. Your Middlers and Juniors may not find it objectionable to do the same things over and over—they may find security in activities that are familiar to them.

I wish *I* felt more secure . . . about how to split up the pupils into small groups, I mean. The rowdy kids want to be in a group together, and then they end up wasting time and cutting up. And the shy kids just sit and look at each other for half their group time before they can get started working together. Any suggestions?

As leader you can always assign groups yourself, mixing the groups as you choose. Whenever you possibly can, however, allow the pupils to volunteer for groups they're interested in. The easiest way to do this is to have sign-up sheets. Indicate on each sheet the maximum number of pupils who may sign up so you don't have nine kids working a crossword puzzle while only two prepare to act out a Bible story. You can always choose groups at random, also—having the pupils draw numbers out of a hat or count off. The key is to vary things as much as you can, but always to do what works best with your kids in your group.

And you know, the kids I lead are . . . well, they're just great kids. I love them all.

What was that—about the kids, I mean?

I love them.

No, what you said before that.

They're great kids.

And when they worship?

What? Oh, I get it! Great kids—GREAT WORSHIP!

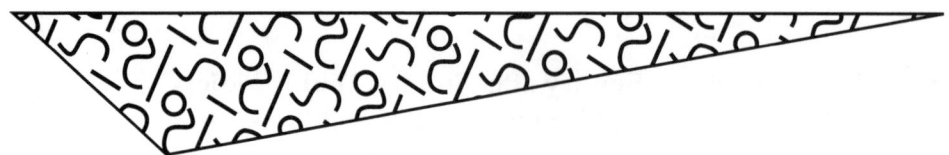

If You've Never Used Great Worship for Kids,

here are some things you need to know:

This book contains 13 sessions. The sessions are based on Scriptures and lessons from Standard Publishing's Middler and Junior Sunday school curriculum.

Each worship session is planned so that pupils work in small groups to prepare the elements of the worship time (call to worship, Scripture, special music, devotion, offering, Lord's Supper, prayer, or personal praise). The elements the small groups have prepared are then incorporated into the worship time.

Each weekly session is designed to last 80-95 minutes. It begins with *Transition Time*, a flexible time between Sunday school and Middler/Junior worship. This is a casual time for relaxation and conversation. It includes a rest room and drink break, as well as a game or activity that allows the children to move around. This freedom is important after the pupils have been sitting during the Sunday school hour.

Involving the children in organized activity as soon as they arrive avoids confusion and eliminates the moments you spend gathering children from the halls when you are ready to begin the worship time.

During *Launching the Theme*, the leader introduces the theme of the session to the children. This is done through a story, object lesson, or dialogue. Involving pupils during this section is a priority. The leader also explains the small group choices and guides the pupils in choosing the groups they are interested in.

Building the Theme is the time when pupils work in their groups to prepare the elements of the worship time. Adult leaders work with the small groups to help them stay on track. Then during *Sharing in Worship* the large group gathers for worship time. An adult leader directs this time and integrates the small group activities so the pupils participate in worship.

Closing Moments is the flexible time between the end of Middler/Junior worship and the end of adult worship. This section lists a variety of activities, but each one can be dropped quickly and easily when the adult service is over.

Activity pages are included with each session plan. You are free to photocopy any of the pages for use with your worship group, but you are NOT permitted to photocopy any of the music that appears in this book. To do so is a violation of copyright.

Worship Plan Sheet

Session _____ Date _____
Unit Title _____
Session Title _____
Scripture Text _____
Worship Focus _____

Transition Time   Leader _____
Materials: _____

Preparation: _____

Procedure: _____
_____
_____

Launching the Theme   Leader _____
Materials: _____

Preparation: _____

Procedure: _____
_____
_____

Building the Theme
Group 1. _____ Leader _____
Materials: _____

Preparation: _____

Procedure: _____
_____
_____

Group 2. _____ Leader _____
Materials: _____

Preparation: _____

Procedure: _____
_____

Group 3. _____ Leader _____
Materials: _____

Preparation: _____
_____

© 1993 by The STANDARD PUBLISHING COMPANY. Permission is granted to photocopy this page for ministry purposes only—not for resale.

Procedure: _____
_____
_____

Group 4. _____ Leader _____
Materials: _____

Preparation: _____
_____

Procedure: _____
_____
_____

Group 5. _____ Leader _____
Materials: _____

Preparation: _____
_____

Procedure: _____
_____
_____

Group 6. _____ Leader _____
Materials: _____

Preparation: _____
_____

Procedure: _____
_____
_____

Sharing in Worship   Leader _____

_____
_____
_____
_____
_____
_____
_____
_____

Closing Moments   Leader _____
Materials: _____

Preparation: _____
_____

Procedure: _____
_____
_____

Unit 1
Leaders Believe God's Promises
Scripture Text: Numbers 13:1, 2, 17-20, 25-28, 30-32;
  14:6-9, 26-28, 30, 31

Session 1

God Promises to Be With Us

Worship Focus

Worship God because He promises to be with us.

Transition Time

(10-15 minutes)

Before the session, prepare a "magnifying glass" for each pupil. To make this, cut a circle 2-3 inches in diameter from construction paper. Attach the circle to a craft stick. On each magnifying glass, write one of the following Scripture references: Deuteronomy 31:8; Joshua 1:9; Jeremiah 1:8; Matthew 28:20b; John 14:3; John 15:4a; Hebrews 13:5b. Prior to the session, hide the completed magnifying glasses throughout the room.

As the pupils arrive, welcome them and encourage each to use the rest room and get a drink. Then involve each pupil in the following activity.

I Spy. Each pupil should be a spy and search the room for a magnifying glass. After a pupil has found one, he should look up the Scripture on his magnifying glass and read it silently.

Launching the Theme

(10 minutes)

After the pupils have had time to locate and read the Scriptures on the magnifying glasses, have them come together as a group.

Each of you was a spy today, first searching the room and then searching God's Word to find a Scripture verse. Our Bible lesson is about some spies. As I tell the story, stand when the spies say something good about the land or that shows they trusted God to be with them. If they didn't trust God, sit down. Raise your hand if your Bible verse has some good advice for the spies.

The people of Israel were camped near the southern border of the land of Canaan. God told Moses to send some men to explore the land of Canaan and bring back a report about the land, the people, the cities, the plants and trees—any information that would prepare the people to take the land God had promised them.

When the spies returned, they gave this report: "The land is a very good land. The soil is fertile for crops. Look at this big cluster of grapes we brought back!" (Pupils stand.) "But the people are huge—they're giants! They are powerful and live in cities with strong walls around them." (Pupils sit. If any raises a hand, choose one to read a

Scripture verse. If none does, ask whether any thinks his or her verse might help.) **Caleb spoke out, "We must take the land. We can do it!"** (Pupils stand.) **Most of the other spies said, "No! We can't attack those people. They're stronger than we are—bigger too!"** (Pupils sit and raise hands. Ask a pupil who has a different Scripture from what was read before to read his or her Scripture.) **At last Joshua and Caleb exclaimed, "Do not rebel against the Lord. The land is good and God is with us. Do not be afraid of these people!"** (Pupils stand.) **Joshua and Caleb remembered God's promise to be with them. Today we will worship God because He keeps His promise to be with us.** (Allow pupils to sit.)

Summarize the activities for *Building the Theme* and allow pupils to choose the groups in which they would like to participate.

Building the Theme
● ● ● ● ● ● ● ● ● ● ● ● ● ● ● ● ● ● ● ●
(30 minutes)

1. Call to Worship. For this activity you will need a poster board or chart paper, markers (two colors), writing paper, pencils, and Bibles. The pupils in this group will write a responsive reading based on Joshua 1:9.

Look up Joshua 1:9 in your Bibles. (Pause while the pupils find it. Have a volunteer read it aloud.) **Today we will use the words, "Be strong and courageous . . . for the Lord your God will be with you wherever you go," to write the Call to Worship.**

Think of times when you need to be strong and courageous or when you need a reminder that God will be with you. Write down several ideas.

After the pupils have done this, help them choose several ideas to use. Use one color of marker to write down an idea, such as, "I'm afraid to go to a new school," or "My friends want me to steal." Under that, write the chosen portion of Joshua 1:9 in the second color of marker. Then write another situation in the first color, followed by the Scripture in the second color. Continue until all ideas chosen have been used. End with the Scripture.

During *Sharing in Worship*, we will read the situations and the large group will read the Scripture. Choose a pupil to lead the large group during *Sharing in Worship*. Practice the responsive reading now.

2. Songs. Provide a variety of hymnals and chorus books for this group. Also provide paper and pencils.

We will use these books to choose some songs for the whole group to sing. Let's look for songs about God's being with us, His faithfulness or friendship to us, or His love and care for us.

Help the pupils select two or three songs for the large group to sing. If the songs are unfamiliar, try to have words and music available for all to use. Practice the songs with these pupils who will lead the songs during *Sharing in Worship*.

3. Offering. Provide the following materials for making a banner: a large piece of burlap or felt, cloth scraps and felt letters, craft glue, glitter, sequins, and a variety of trims. Also provide a dowel rod and yarn or rope for hanging the banner. A new banner will be made each Sunday of this unit.

Today we will make a banner praising God for promising to be with us. The banner will remind us today and in the next few weeks what a wonderful God we have.

The pupils will present the banner at offering time during *Sharing in Worship*. Ask for volunteers to pray for and collect the offering.

4. Scripture. Each pupil will need a copy of Activity Page 1A, a pencil, and a Bible.

Look up each Scripture on your activity page. Read the Scripture. Then put the Scripture in your own words about a time when that Scripture might be helpful to you. The first one has been done for you as an example.

During *Sharing in Worship*, a volunteer will read a Scripture from his Bible and then read his application of it. If you do not get a volunteer for each Scripture and application, read that Scripture yourself and suggest an application.

5. Devotion. Each pupil will need a copy of Activity Page 1B, a Bible, and a pencil. Props, such as clipboards and a microphone, would be helpful.

Your activity page has a radio interview to review today's Bible story. Open your Bibles to Numbers 13. Let's work together to complete the blanks in the interview. We will refer to the Scriptures given on the activity page to check our facts.

After the blanks have been filled in, let volunteers take the parts of the interviewer and those interviewed. Practice the interview, complete with props, if desired.

6. Prayer. Provide chart paper and markers for this group to make a prayer chart that will be used throughout this unit.

For the next few weeks, we will be talking about how God keeps His promises. One of those promises is that He hears and answers our prayers. We will make a prayer chart on which we can record the prayer requests and answered prayers for our entire group. We need to have space for the date, the request, and the answer to the prayer.

The pupils in this group may list their prayer requests or answers to prayer now. During *Sharing in Worship* they will add requests made by the other pupils and leaders. Each week the chart will be updated.

Sharing in Worship
(20-25 minutes)

Omit any of the following sections if you did not offer the corresponding activity.

Call to Worship (Group 1): **The pupils in Group 1 will lead us in a responsive reading. They will read the sentences in (color). Then we will read the Scripture in (color).** Let Group 1 lead the reading.

Songs (Group 2): **Group 2 chose some songs to remind us that God is with us. Let's sing with them.** Group 2 leads the singing.

Offering (Group 3): **Group 3 designed a praise banner as an offering of their talents to the Lord.** Group 3 will show and explain the banner. The volunteers will pray and pass the offering containers.

Lord's Supper: God loves us very much. He has promised to be with us. Even better than that, He has made a place for us in Heaven so we can be with Him. We all sin, however, and our sin keeps us from being with God. But God planned a way for our sin to be forgiven so that we could be with Him.

Listen to what God says in Romans 5:6-8. (Read it.) **Because Jesus died a horrible death on the cross, God will forgive our sins. Then He can be with us here on earth and we can be with Him in Heaven forever. Let's think about God's great love for us in sending Jesus to die. Let's pray together and thank God for Jesus.**

Scripture (Group 4): **Group 4 would like to read some Scriptures and tell us how they can apply the Scriptures.** Group 4 reads Scriptures and applications.

Devotion (Group 5): **Group 5 has prepared an interview for us.** Group 5 performs their interview.

How many of the spies in today's Bible story can you name without looking them up? (Allow time for answers.) **Joshua and Caleb are the only ones I can remember. Perhaps that is because Joshua and Caleb were the only ones who remembered God's promise to be with them.**

What a wonderful place the land of Canaan must have been! Fertile land with abundant crops, flowing with milk and honey, they said! But there were cities well fortified and strong people who seemed like giants. How easy it would be to feel like a grasshopper in a land where giants roamed and a cluster of grapes took two men to carry!

We probably would react the way most of the spies reacted. We would think the task of taking the land to be an impossible one. But that's because we often think of doing things all by ourselves. We forget that God has promised to be with us.

When we think we can't do right because our friends would laugh or some bully would pound on us, we need to remember that God is with us. Our friends may laugh and the bully may beat us up, but God will give us the strength to do right and put up with what the people around us do.

Jesus gave us a wonderful promise in John 16:33. He said, "I have told you these things, so that in me you may have peace. In this world you will have trouble. But take heart! I have overcome the world." He knew we would have trouble, but because He is with us, we can get through it! He has overcome the world!

Prayer (Group 6): Group 6 has prepared a prayer chart for us to use this month. Group 6 will explain the prayer chart and fill in requests and answers mentioned now. You may want to take a few moments to talk about the ways God answers prayers. Children, as well as adults, need to be reminded from time to time that God may answer "No," or "Wait awhile." These are answers, even though they may not be the ones we are seeking! A volunteer or leader may close with prayer.

Closing Moments
(10-15 minutes)

Distribute copies of Activity Page 1C and pencils to the pupils. Each pupil also will need a Bible. Let the pupils work on the crossword puzzle until time to go.

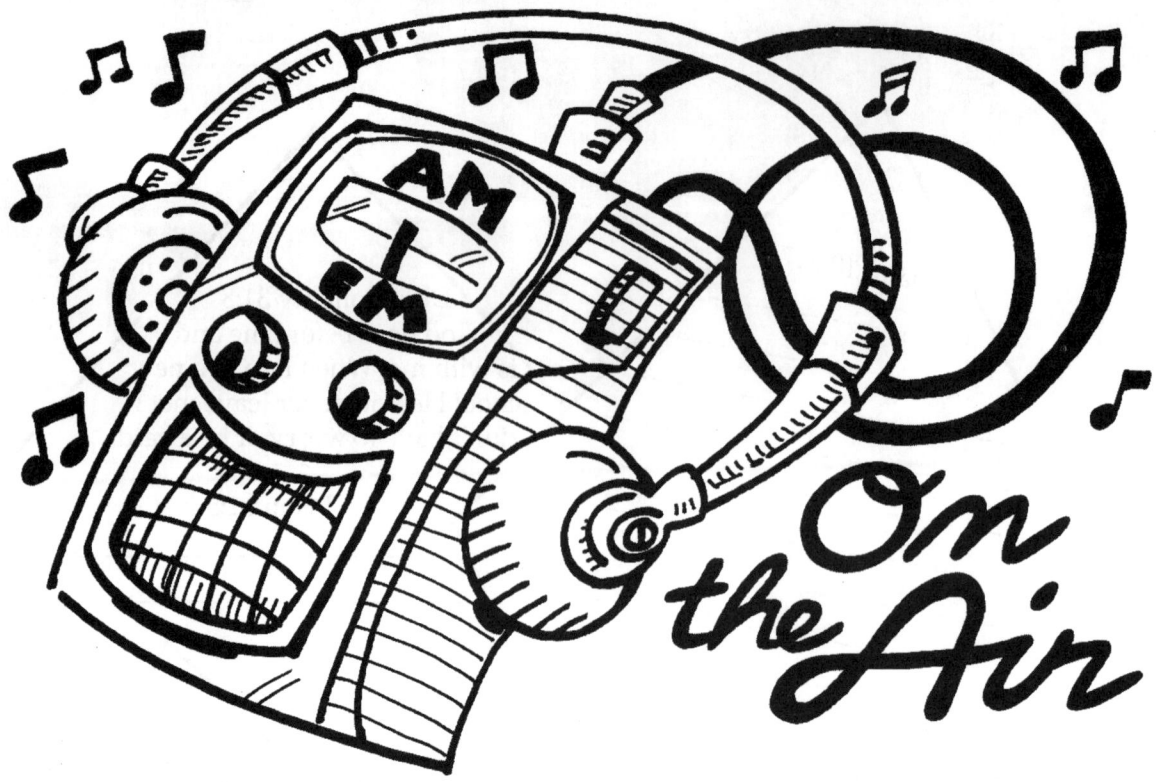

The news crew from WCAN radio interviewed some of the spies and onlookers from Numbers 13, 14. Complete the interview in your own words. Then choose parts and practice the interview.

HANNAH: This is Hannah from **WCAN** radio news. The spies Moses sent out have just returned from the land of Canaan and we're here with an exclusive report. . . . Excuse me, sir. You were one of the spies. What did the land look like?

SPY #1 (Numbers 13:27):
_____
_____
_____

HANNAH: Wow! Look at those grapes! Too bad this isn't television! How about you, sir? What did you think?

SPY #2 (Numbers 13:28):
_____
_____
_____

CALEB (interrupting): Wait! Let me tell you about it!

HANNAH: Were you one of the spies also? What is your name, and what do you have to say?

CALEB: My name is Caleb. Here's what I think (Numbers 13:30):
_____
_____
_____
_____

SEVERAL SPIES (Numbers 13:31-33):
_____
_____
_____
_____

HANNAH: Well, I guess that about wraps it up. The majority opinion is that the land is great, but the people who live there are such strong and big people that it is impossible for anyone to take over the land of Canaan.

JOSHUA and CALEB: No! The land is wonderful, and we can take it. If the Lord is pleased with us, He will give it to us! We must not rebel against God. He is with us and we must not be afraid to take the land!

HANNAH: I must say, Joshua and Caleb certainly are insistent! I think this situation bears watching. We will have updates on this story as the news breaks. For now, this is Hannah from **WCAN** radio signing off.

Crossword Review

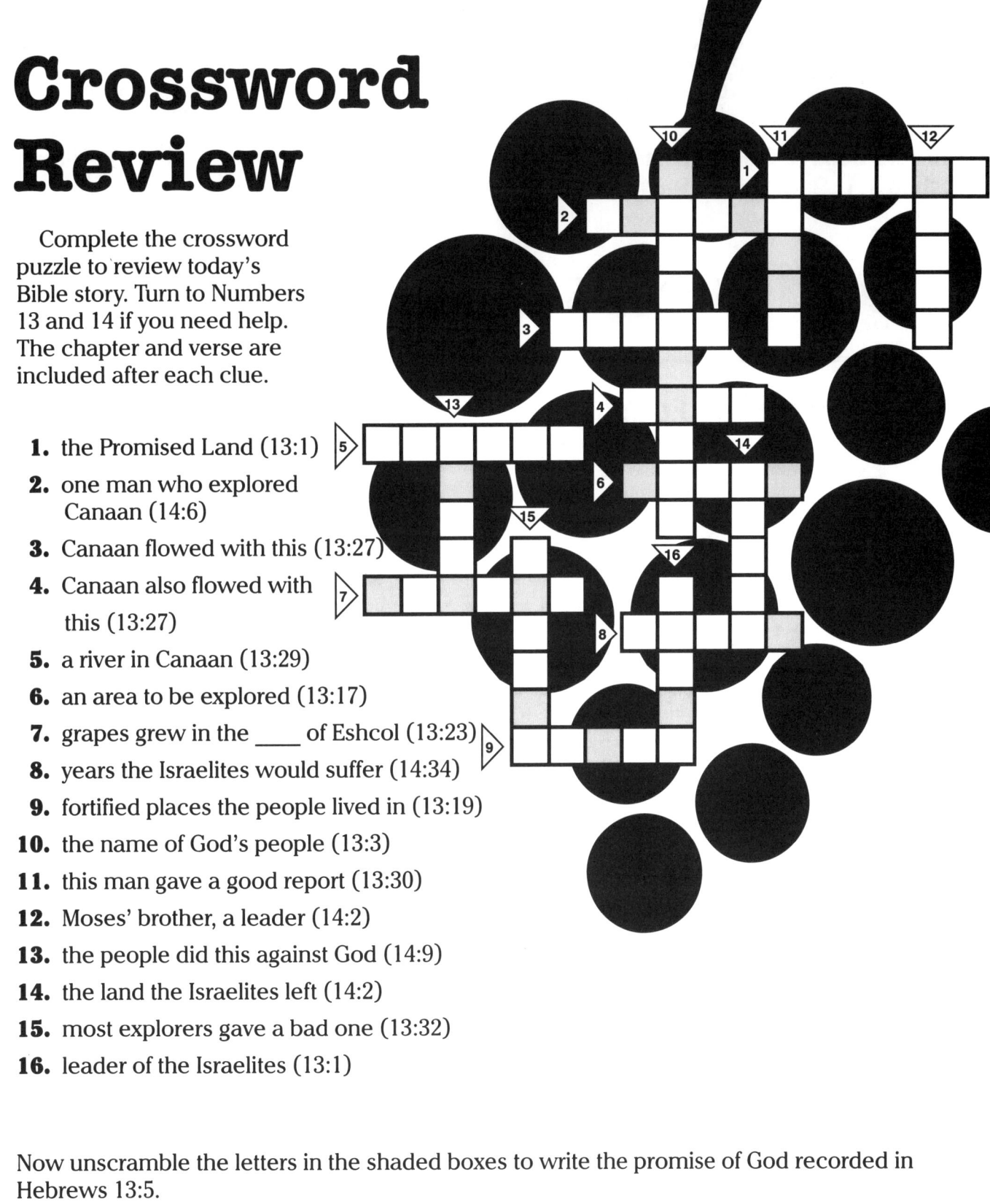

Complete the crossword puzzle to review today's Bible story. Turn to Numbers 13 and 14 if you need help. The chapter and verse are included after each clue.

1. the Promised Land (13:1)
2. one man who explored Canaan (14:6)
3. Canaan flowed with this (13:27)
4. Canaan also flowed with this (13:27)
5. a river in Canaan (13:29)
6. an area to be explored (13:17)
7. grapes grew in the ___ of Eshcol (13:23)
8. years the Israelites would suffer (14:34)
9. fortified places the people lived in (13:19)
10. the name of God's people (13:3)
11. this man gave a good report (13:30)
12. Moses' brother, a leader (14:2)
13. the people did this against God (14:9)
14. the land the Israelites left (14:2)
15. most explorers gave a bad one (13:32)
16. leader of the Israelites (13:1)

Now unscramble the letters in the shaded boxes to write the promise of God recorded in Hebrews 13:5.

___ ___ ___ ___ ___ ___ ___ ___ ___
___ ___ ___ ___ ___ ___ ___ ___.

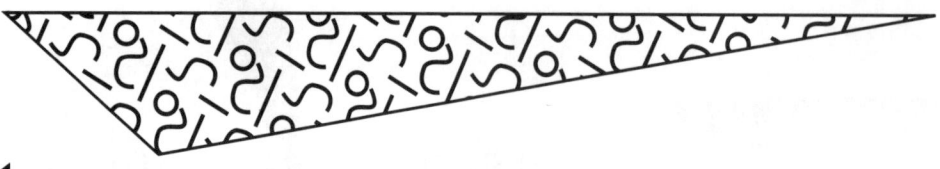

Unit 1
Leaders Believe God's Promises
Joshua 1:1: 2; 6:1, 2, 6, 9-11, 14-16, 20

Session 2

God Promises to Protect Us

Worship Focus

Worship God because He promises to protect us.

Transition Time

(10-15 minutes)

Greet the pupils as they arrive and welcome any newcomers. Send them in small groups to the rest rooms and drinking fountain. Involve everyone in the following activity.

Protection Montage. Provide magazines, coloring books, Sunday school papers and visual materials, glue, scissors, and a sheet of paper large enough for the pupils to work together on a montage.

Look through these materials for pictures of people who need protection, especially people who need the kind of protection the Lord can give. Cut out the pictures and glue them to the large paper in any way you want. If you find a picture of someone who is being protected, cut that out and glue it to the center of the paper.

Launching the Theme

(10 minutes)

While the pupils work, arrange your chairs in a square, facing in. This will be "Jericho." When the montage is completed, discuss it briefly. Then display it on a wall or bulletin board. Gather the pupils together in a corner of the room.

Here we are! We've made it across the Jordan River. Now let's go get the land God promised us was ours. Uh-oh! Have you seen Jericho? There's a wall all around the city. We can't get in that place! It's shut up tight! They must have known we were coming. Now how will we take over the city?

Shh! What's that Joshua is saying? We're going to walk around the city? We have to be quiet? The trumpets will play, but we can't say a word! Well, I don't know what good that will do, but Joshua said the Lord told him to do this. Let's get in line behind the others. (Lead the pupils around the city.)

Just as I thought! Nothing happened. At least we should sleep well tonight after that hike. (Pause briefly.)

Not again! Just like yesterday, we have to walk around Jericho with trumpets blaring and not utter a word. Let's go! (Go around again. Keep everyone silent. Repeat the process with similar conversation to indicate that this goes on for a total of six days.)

Here we are again! Six days we marched around Jericho. The people must think we're crazy by now! Joshua says the Lord wants us to go around the city seven times today! The people from Jericho will surely attack us when we go around so many times! When Joshua tells us to, we're supposed to shout. I guess we might as well go on and try it. The Lord has taken care of us so far.

We're almost done with our seventh time. Joshua is telling us to shout. (Shout with the pupils. Each of you should grab a chair, fold it up, and lay it down [or turn it over] to represent the walls collapsing.) **Look! The walls are down. God has given us the city! He has protected us! Praise God! Praise the Lord for His protection!**

Summarize the activities for *Building the Theme* and allow pupils to choose the groups in which they would like to participate. Try to have groups that are even in size. Before the pupils go to their groups, enlist their aid in setting up and arranging the chairs for worship.

Building the Theme
● ● ● ● ● ● ● ● ● ● ● ● ● ● ● ● ● ● ● ●
(30 minutes)

1. Call to worship. Provide Bibles, poster paper, and pencils or markers for the pupils.

Turn to Psalm 18:1-3. (A volunteer should read after all have found the Scripture.) **For today's Call to Worship, we will read the Scripture and do motions to it. Let's decide how we can act out the Scripture.**

After the motions are decided, let the pupils print the Scripture on the poster board. Then practice reading the Scripture and doing the motions. The pupils may illustrate the poster with the motions if time allows. A volunteer or leader will hold the poster so Group 1 can read it and act out the motions.

2. Offering. Provide the following materials for making a banner: a large piece of burlap or felt, cloth scraps and felt letters, craft glue, glitter, sequins, and a variety of trims. Also provide a dowel rod and yarn or rope for hanging the banner. A new banner will be made each Sunday of this unit.

Today we will make a banner praising God for promising to protect us. The banner will remind us today and in the next few weeks what a wonderful God we have.

The pupils will present the banner at offering time during *Sharing in Worship.* Ask for volunteers to pray for and collect the offering.

3. Special Music. Provide writing paper and pencils or pens for the pupils. Bibles with concordances should also be available.

Today we will write a song praising God for protecting us. First we must choose a tune for our song. (Suggest several choruses or hymns that the pupils know. A song such as "London Bridge" or "Row, Row, Row Your Boat" would also work. Let the pupils help make the decision.)

Now let's work on the words to the song. Write a poem that fits our tune. (Pupils may use the Bibles to find verses that might work for the song. For example: Psalms 3:3-5; 16:1, 7, 8, 11; 17:6, 8; 18:1-3.)

Allow pupils time to write stanzas for the song. Then read them aloud. Choose a few to sing and practice. The song could also be written cooperatively instead of as individual stanzas.

4. Devotion. Provide writing materials and Bibles for the pupils.

Let's write a newspaper article about today's Bible story. Turn in your Bibles to the book of Joshua. We will read chapters 1 and 6:1-20. That will give us the background for our story. As you

read silently, think of questions that a newspaper reporter might ask. **Especially be looking for ways God protected His people.**

Help the pupils as necessary in writing one or more articles about the conquest of Jericho. Give the newspaper a name and include headlines. Perhaps someone could draw a picture to illustrate the story. The newspaper could also have an advice column and a weather report. Encourage the pupils' imaginations, but remind them to report the truth accurately. Check their work for any errors or omissions

The newspaper will be read during the Devotion. Assign sections to all who are willing to read aloud. Let the pupils practice reading their sections aloud now.

5. Personal Praise. Each pupil will need a Bible, a copy of Activity Page 2A, and a pencil.

Throughout the book of Psalms we find poems that David or other poets wrote about God's protection. Let's look at a few. They are listed on your activity page. (Look up each passage and read it aloud.) **Use these ideas or some of your own to write a poem praising God for His promise to protect us.**

After the pupils have completed their poems, have them read their poems to the group. All who are willing will read poems during *Sharing in Worship*.

6. Prayer. Provide the prayer chart used last week and markers. Each pupil will need a Bible, a copy of Activity Page 2B, and a pencil.

Look at our prayer chart from last week. Does anyone have any request to add to the chart or any answer to prayer to fill in? (Update the chart.)

Throughout the Bible we can read prayers prayed by some of God's people. One example is sometimes called the Lord's Prayer. It is the model Jesus used to teach His disciples how to pray. Let's read Matthew 6:9-13. In this prayer, we can see praises and requests, including a request for protection from evil.

On your activity page, write a prayer, beginning with praise to God. Then you may write some requests. Include some of the people on our prayer chart. We will use these prayers to lead the large group in prayer.

Sharing in Worship
(20-25 minutes)

Omit any of the following sections if you did not offer the corresponding activity.

Call to Worship (Group 1): **Group 1 has a special call to worship this morning.** Group 1 reads their Scripture and uses the motions they planned.

Songs: Lead the group in some praise songs. Include songs from last week.

Offering (Group 2): **Group 2 has a new banner as a talent offering.** Group 2 shows and explains their banner. Volunteers pray and receive the offering.

Lord's Supper: The Bible tells us, "All have sinned" (Romans 3:23). **But even when Adam and Eve sinned, God already had a plan to protect us from our sins. Listen to what God said in Genesis 3:15.** (Read it.) **God already planned for Jesus to die on the cross so that our sins could be forgiven. Let's thank God for letting Jesus take our sins so we could be forgiven.** Pray and serve the Lord's Supper.

Special Music (Group 3): **Group 3 has written a song to help us praise God.** Group 3 sings. If time allows, Group 3 may teach the song to the large group.

Devotion (Group 4): **The pupils in Group 4 were newspaper reporters. They will share their newspaper with us now.** After Group 4 reads their newspaper, add any important information that may have been left out.

God protected the pupils of Israel, and He will protect us. There are several ways that God protects. First, He has given us the Bible to help us know what is right and good. The Bible guides us and helps us know God so we can try to be like Him. When we live the way God wants us to, we can avoid many bad decisions that would lead us to harm.

Another way God protects us is by giving us parents and families. (If you have pupils who live with grandparents or other parent substitutes, mention these too.) The people who love us take care of us and help us to avoid things that are wrong. They keep us from danger.

Another way God protects us is through Christian leaders and teachers. They help us to learn God's way and encourage us to follow it.

God gives us His Word and many people to protect us. They also comfort us when things do go wrong or when something bad happens, such as a sickness, an accident, or a death. Giving us comfort is another way God protects us.

Personal Praise (Group 5): **Because God protects us, we want to praise Him. The pupils in Group 5 have written some praise poems they would like to share with us.** Group 5 reads their poems now.

Prayer (Group 6): **Group 6 will help us update our prayer chart from last week.** Allow Group 6 to write in requests and prayer answers. Comment as needed. Then Group 6 will close by reading the prayers they wrote earlier.

Closing Moments
(10-15 minutes)

Each pupil will need a Bible, a pencil, and a copy of Activity Page 2C. Allow the pupils to decode the message on the activity page. The answer is, "God is our refuge and strength, an ever-present help in trouble. Therefore we will not fear" (Psalm 46:1, 2a).

If several pupils finish before their parents come, let them choose another Bible verse to encode, using the same code. Then other pupils can decode that message. This could also be done on a chalkboard so that the entire group could decode the message.

Pen a Praise Poem

The book of Psalms is full of poems. Look up these Psalms that talk about God's protection.

Psalm 3:3-6   Psalm 18:1-3   Psalm 27:1, 14
Psalm 28:6-9   Psalm 46:1-3   Psalm 56:1-3, 9-11

Now write your own poem praising God for His protection. Use the lines below.

Write a Prayer

When we write a prayer, we can read it again later to see how God is answering. Write a prayer today. Be sure to include praise to God. Also make requests for those who are on your prayer list.

Secret Code

Use the code to figure out the message. After you have decoded it, choose another Bible verse to put into code (the same code or one you make up). Then let a friend decipher your message.

Code Key: For each letter in the coded message, substitute the letter that is two letters before it in the alphabet. If the code says E, the real letter is C. If the code says A, the real letter is Y.

Code:

IQF KU QWT TGHWIG CPF UVTGPIVJ, CP

___

GXGT-RTGUGPV JGNR KP VTQWDNG. VJGTGHQTG

___

YG YKNN PQV HGCT. —Psalm 46:1, 2a

___

Unit 1
Leaders Believe God's Promises
Scripture Text: Joshua 24:1-7, 11, 13-18, 26, 27

Session 3

God's Word Promises Guidance

Worship Focus

Worship God because God's Word promises guidance.

Transition Time

(10-15 minutes)

As the pupils arrive, welcome them and encourage each to use the rest room and get a drink. Then involve each pupil in the following activity.

Treasure Hunt. Prior to the session, prepare instructions for a treasure hunt within your classroom, building (but not where others might be disturbed), or even outdoors if your climate permits. Give directions such as, "Go to the fifth chair from the left in the first row," or "Go out the door of the classroom. Turn left. Go past three doors. Go in the next door. Look under the first cabinet on the right." Then at that location, have another instruction leading to another place. If you intend to use more than one group of pupils, try to place the instruction sites where they cannot be seen from other instruction sites. Do not make your locations easy to guess without reading the clues.

Continue through several steps leading to a small prize for the pupils (bookmarks, pencils, candy). The entire group can move together or the pupils can be grouped in groups of five or less. Prepare sets of directions for as many groups as you anticipate. (If later instructions will be left at their sites, only one of each will be needed.) Start the groups at different times. As each group reaches the final destination, distribute prizes.

Launching the Theme

(10 minutes)

Gather the pupils in your meeting place and talk about the treasure hunt.

Treasure hunts are fun, aren't they? How did you know where to go? (Allow responses.) **That's right. You were given instructions to guide you. Sometimes you might have been tempted to go your own way because you thought you knew where the path was leading, but without following the guide, you couldn't be sure you would end up in the right place.**

The children of Israel were on a type of treasure hunt. In today's Bible story, Joshua reminds the people of their history and the One who had guided them—God.

Many years before this, Abraham and his family had left where they were living and traveled throughout the land of Canaan. Later Jacob and his family went to Egypt where the Hebrews lived for a long time, finally becoming slaves.

God sent Moses and Aaron to Pharaoh as His spokesmen. Pharaoh refused to listen throughout the plagues God sent. Finally, after all the firstborn in Egypt were killed, Pharaoh sent the people of Israel away. They went from Egypt to the land God had promised them, wandering in the wilderness for a long time.

Joshua reminded the people of the many ways God guided them and challenged them to continue to serve the Lord. Today we will worship God because He has promised to guide us through His Word.

Summarize the activities for *Building the Theme* and allow pupils to choose the groups in which they would like to participate. Try to have an equal number of pupils in each group.

Building the Theme
(30 minutes)

1. Call to Worship. Provide Bibles, poster board, and drawing materials, including scratch paper. Pupils will make a rebus to use for the Call to Worship.

Locate Psalm 119 in your Bibles. This Psalm is 176 verses long! Every verse is about God's Word. Sometimes God's Word is referred to as law, decrees, commands, or statutes. Today we will read several of these verses. Then we will choose one or two for the Call to Worship. To help the other pupils read it, we will draw a rebus of the verse. You may need to explain that a rebus is a message made up of words and pictures of words.

Read Psalm 119:1, 2, 11, 33, 34, 89, 90. Help the pupils consider which of these verses to use for the Call to Worship. Then help them decide which words to letter and which ones to illustrate. Have them sketch their rebus on scratch paper first.

After the rebus is done, practice reading it together until it goes smoothly. Enlist a volunteer who will explain the rebus to the large group before the rebus is read together.

2. Songs. Provide a variety of song books, hymnals, and chorus books for this group. Also provide paper and pencils.

We will use these books to choose some songs for the whole group to sing. Let's look for songs about God's Word. We also want to find songs that talk about God's guidance—how He leads us.

Help the pupils select two or three appropriate songs for the large group to sing. If the songs are unfamiliar, try to have words and music available for all to use. Practice the songs with these pupils who will lead the songs during *Sharing in Worship*.

3. Offering. Provide the following materials for making a banner: a large piece of burlap or felt, cloth scraps and felt letters, craft glue, glitter, sequins, and a variety of trims. Also provide a dowel rod and yarn or rope for hanging the banner. A new banner will be made each Sunday of this unit.

Today we will make a banner praising God because His Word promises guidance. The banner will remind us today and in the next few weeks what a wonderful God we have and how He guides us with His Word.

The pupils will present the banner at offering time during *Sharing in Worship*. Ask for volunteers to pray for and collect the offering.

4. Scripture. Provide Bibles and art materials for this activity.

Turn to Joshua 24 in your Bibles. As I read some verses from this chapter, listen for ways that God guided His people. We will choose several scenes from Joshua's speech to illustrate. This will help our entire group worship God for guiding His people. If you want, print the Scripture Text on the chalkboard ahead of time to help the pupils follow along in their Bibles as you read.

Read Joshua 24:1-7, 11, 13-18, 26, 27 slowly. Then discuss with the pupils a few scenes to illustrate. Help them as needed with ideas. Then let the pupils rehearse displaying and explaining their pictures. Keep the pictures in chronological order.

5. Devotion. Pupils will need index cards, pencils, Bibles, and concordances.

The Israelites needed God's help and guidance. They received this through messengers from God—chiefly, Moses, Aaron, and Joshua.

We also need God to guide us, but we don't have leaders, such as Moses or Joshua, through whom God can speak. Although we can't hear God speak, His words are written in the Bible to guide us. He has given us the Bible so that we can read His words again and again.

Sometimes we are tempted to do wrong. Can God's Word guide us? Of course, it can! Sometimes we feel sad or afraid. Can God's Word guide us? Definitely! Sometimes we are having a hard time knowing whether or not something would please God. Can God's Word help us then? Yes!

Let's think of times when we need God's Word to guide us. We will use these situations, and answers from the Bible, to do some role plays. These ideas will help the other pupils in our large group to see how God's Word promises to be our guide.

Help the pupils think of ideas and locate Scriptures that would help them. They can record their ideas and the Scriptures on index cards. Then help them to perform role plays based on the ideas and Scriptures. Practice the role plays as much as time allows.

6. Prayer. Provide the prayer chart from the previous weeks, markers, copies of Activity Page 3A, construction paper, staplers, and pencils. In order for everyone in the class to have a prayer journal, you will need at least two copies of the activity page for each pupil.

Update the prayer chart used in previous weeks. Add new requests and answers. More will be added during *Sharing in Worship*.

Prayer should be a very important part of our lives. When we write down our prayers, we can keep track of them better. Then we can see how God answers them. We can also remember requests better. In addition to that, we can see how we are maturing in our relationship with the Lord.

Sometimes we may want to write out our entire prayer. Other times we may just want to record our requests in a few words. Then we can add the date and answer or update that request easily. For both of these ways of keeping track of our prayers, it is helpful to have a prayer journal.

Many of you have kept a journal or a diary for school or for your own enjoyment. A prayer journal is similar to that. It is a private record of your talks with God. Today we will make prayer journals for ourselves and the others in our large group. Then we can all make our time with the Lord even more special.

Provide at least two copies of the activity page and a piece of construction paper for each pupil in this small group. Also provide scissors, markers for decorating the cover, and staplers. After each pupil has made a journal for himself, let him make another. Let the pupils make as many as they can. Encourage them to work quickly but also to be neat.

Prayer journals will be distributed at the beginning of prayer time during *Sharing in Worship*.

Sharing in Worship
(20-25 minutes)

Omit any of the following sections if you did not offer the corresponding activity.

Call to Worship (Group 1): **Group 1 has a special way for us to read our Scripture today.** Group 1 explains the rebus and leads the large group in reading it.

Songs (Group 2): **Group 2 has chosen some songs to help us praise God for guiding us.** Group 2 leads singing.

Offering (Group 3): **Group 3 designed a praise banner as an offering of their talents to the Lord.** Group 3 will show and explain the banner. The volunteers will pray and pass the offering containers.

Lord's Supper: God gave the Israelites many ways to remember His goodness to them and His guidance. Often He used feasts and ceremonies as reminders. Each week we have a reminder of God's goodness to us. We have the Lord's Supper as a celebration of Jesus' death so that our sins could be forgiven. Let's praise God now for this special reminder of His love.

Scripture (Group 4): **Group 4 will show us some ways that God guided the Israelites.** Group 4 will show and explain their illustrations of the Bible story.

Devotion (Group 5): **Group 5 will help us see some ways that God guides us through His Word, the Bible.** Group 5 acts out role plays. After each role play, discuss it briefly, adding any insights you have into the situation and also tying in any other Scriptures you think of that fit the situation.

Sometimes we may think that God's Word can't have answers to guide us in today's world. It is true that God's Word won't tell us which television show to watch or which friends to have. However, if we hide God's Word in our hearts, that is, memorize it, we will find that it can guide us. The principles, the ideas, in the Bible are true for all time—from Bible times until Jesus comes again. By knowing what God says, we can choose wisely to do right.

Prayer (Group 6): **Group 6 prepared prayer journals for us. These journals can help us keep track of our prayer requests and answers. We can also record our praise to God.** Group 6 will distribute the prayer journals. Then the pupils will update the prayer chart. Encourage the pupils to record items from the prayer chart in their journals. Close with prayer.

Closing Moments
(10-15 minutes)

Provide copies of Activity Page 3B and pencils. Pupils will complete the maze by following the phrases that describe God's Word.

NOTE: You will need an older teenage girl or a woman, dressed in a Bible-times costume if possible, to play the part of Deborah during *Launching the Theme* for next week. See page 29 for more details.

Prayer Journal

Cut on the black lines. Put the pages together and fold on the dotted line. Make a cover from construction paper, and assemble the book. Staple the pages together at the fold.

Date	Request	Answer	Date	Request	Answer

cut across ←

Date	Request	Answer	Date	Request	Answer

© 1994 by The STANDARD PUBLISHING COMPANY. Permission is granted to photocopy this page for ministry purposes only—not for resale.

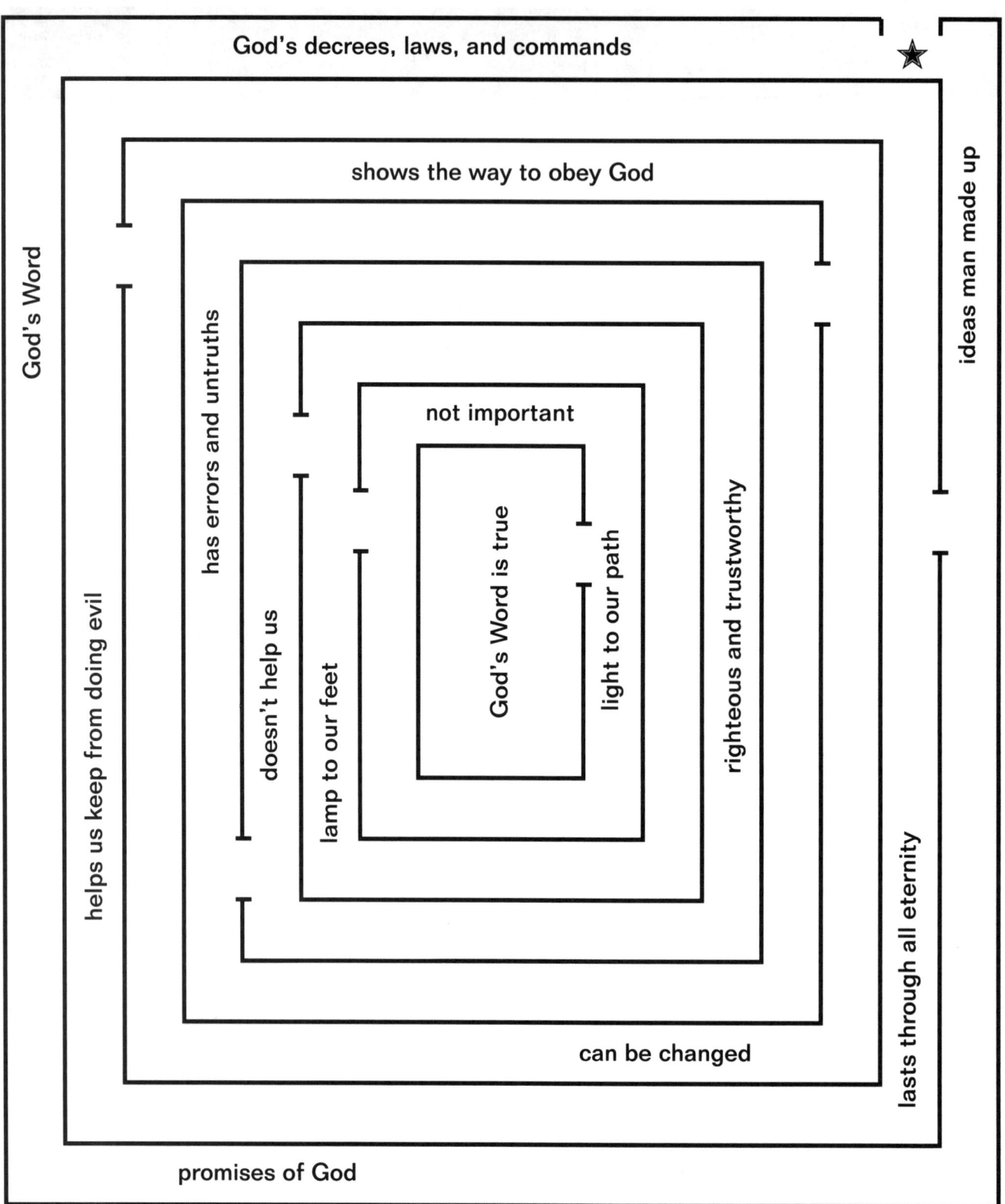

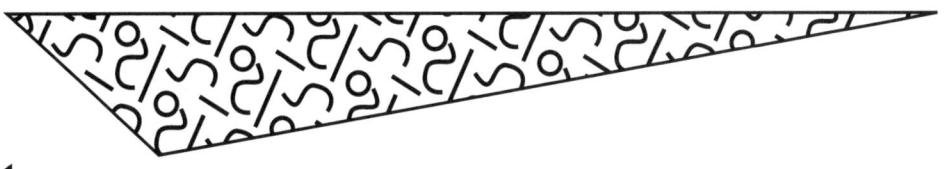

Unit 1
Leaders Believe God's Promises
Scripture Text: Judges 4:1-10, 12-16, 23

Session 4

God Promises to Answer Our Prayers

Worship Focus

Worship God because He promises to answer our prayers.

Transition Time

(10-15 minutes)

As the children arrive, welcome them and encourage each to use the rest room and get a drink. Then involve each child in the following activity.

Telephone. Have the children sit in a circle. Each circle should have between seven and fifteen children. Choose a pupil in each group to be the starter. Whisper a question to each starter (preferably the same question). The starter should whisper the question to the person on his right. The question is whispered from person to person around the circle until it gets to the person sitting immediately to the left of the starter. That person hears the question and then whispers an answer to the person on his left. The answer continues around the circle to the left until it has been whispered to the starter.

At that time the last person to hear the question asks the question. Then the starter gives the answer he heard. Compare these to the original question and the original answer.

Launching the Theme

(10 minutes)

Ahead of time, ask an older teenage girl or a woman to dress in a Bible-times costume and play the part of Deborah. Give her a copy of the script that follows, or let her talk for herself, based on Judges 4:1-10, 12-16, 23. If it is impossible to have a guest, tell the story in your own words.

Gather the children together in a large group. **What a difference there was between the original question and the way it ended! That also affected the answer that was given, didn't it? Isn't it wonderful that God hears our prayers accurately all the time? Even better than that, God always knows the best way to answer our prayers and He does that at just the right time!**

Today we have a guest who can tell us about a time when God answered the prayers of His people, the Israelites. Hello, Deborah. We're glad you could be with us today.

Deborah speaks: **My people, the Israelites, had prayed to the Lord for many, many years asking Him for help. Jabin, a king, and Sisera, the commander of his army, had been treating us cruelly for twenty years.**

At last the Lord told me it was time. He would give Jabin, Sisera, and their army into our hands. I was a prophetess in Israel at that time. I was also a judge.

One day the Lord told me to send for Barak. I told him that God wanted him to lead an army to attack Sisera. In fact, God would lure Sisera and his army to Barak and give Sisera into Barak's hands.

Barak was unsure and wanted me to go with him. I told him I would, but that God would hand Sisera over to a woman.

The Lord gave Barak the victory over Sisera's army, but Sisera escaped. A woman named Jael killed him. From that time on, King Jabin did not bother us. The Lord had answered our prayers—even though it took twenty years. God knew when it was the right time.

Thank Deborah and allow her to leave. **Today we will worship God because He promises to answer our prayers.**

Summarize the activities for *Building the Theme* and allow pupils to choose the groups in which they would like to participate. Try to have an equal number of pupils in each group.

Building the Theme
(30 minutes)

1. Call to Worship. Provide Bibles (all the same version) for the pupils.

Turn in your Bibles to Psalm 34:15 and 17a. Let's read this aloud together. Today we will memorize these verses and say them as a chant for our Call to Worship. Begin saying the verses together. Practice until the pupils have the verses memorized. Then rehearse the verses by saying them softly the first time, slightly louder a second time, and louder a third time. Remind the children that talking louder does not mean shouting. Those listening should be able to understand the words. The reason for increasing volume is for emphasis. The pupils should speak with feeling also.

2. Personal Praise. Provide Bibles, copies of Activity Page 4A, and pencils for the pupils. Prior to the session, complete one or two words or phrases of an acrostic to show the pupils how to complete an acrostic.

Today we will praise God because He answers our prayers. Each of us will use the words *God answers prayers* as an acrostic to write praise words or phrases. On your activity page you see the letters going down the center of the page. You may use any of the letters as the beginning, middle, or end of your words and phrases. Your words could come from Bible verses about prayer. They could be from prayer requests you have made, which God has answered. The words could just be praises because God promises to answer our prayers.

Allow pupils time to complete their acrostics. Provide guidance, but do not complete the acrostics for them. Pupils will read their acrostics individually during *Sharing in Worship.* After all acrostics are read, the pupils should say together, "God answers prayers." Rehearse the reading and response.

3. Special Music. Provide Bibles, writing paper, and pencils.

Look up Judges 4:1-10, 12-16, and 23 in your Bibles. Listen carefully while I read these verses aloud. (Do so.) **Let's write a song about this Bible story. We want to tell the exciting parts, especially that God answered the prayers of the Israelites. First, let's choose a tune for our song.**

Help the pupils decide on a familiar tune—a hymn, chorus, simple children's tune. Then help them write two or three stanzas to review the Bible story. Emphasize the fact that God answers prayers, even though He sometimes says, "Wait."

Rehearse the song. If you wish to teach it to the large group, have pupils write the words on poster board.

4. Offering. Provide the following materials for making a banner: a large piece of burlap or felt, cloth scraps and felt letters, craft glue, glitter, sequins, and a variety of trims. Also provide a dowel rod and yarn or rope for hanging the banner. A different banner has been made each Sunday of this unit.

Today we will make a banner praising God because He promises to answer our prayers. The banner will remind us what a wonderful God we have and how He always hears and answers prayers.

The children will present the banner at Offering time during *Sharing in Worship*. Ask for volunteers to pray for and collect the offering.

5. Scripture. Provide Bibles, copies of Activity Page 4B, and pencils.

Let's do a Scripture search today. We will find out what some verses in the Bible tell us about God's hearing and answering our prayers.

Allow pupils time to look up the Scriptures and put them in their own words. A few words are given to help them get started. If some pupils have difficulty paraphrasing Scripture, ask a few questions to get them to explain the verses to you orally. Then suggest they write what they told you.

Have a volunteer read and explain each Scripture. Rehearse this so pupils will feel comfortable doing that during *Sharing in Worship*.

6. Prayer. Provide the prayer chart and markers. Also provide thank-you note cards and pencils for the pupils.

Let's bring our prayer chart up to date. Review previous requests and answers. Add any new information, requests, answers, and praises.

God is so wonderful to listen to our prayers. No matter when we talk to Him or what we pray about, He hears us and He answers our prayers. The Holy Spirit even helps us when we don't know exactly how to pray! Read Romans 8:26, 27.

Let's write thank-you notes to God for hearing and answering our prayers. Allow pupils time to do so. Ask for volunteers who will read their thank-you notes during the prayer time.

Sharing in Worship
● ●
(20-25 minutes)

Omit any of the following sections if you did not offer the corresponding activity.

Call to Worship (Group 1): **Group 1 has a Scripture to share with us.** Group 1 chants Psalm 34:15 and 17a.

Songs: Lead the pupils in a few songs, especially ones about God's hearing our prayers.

Personal Praise (Group 2): **Group 2 wants to praise God for answering our prayers.** Group 2 reads their acrostics and says, "God answers prayers."

Special Music (Group 3): **Group 3 has written a song.** Group 3 sings the song they wrote, and then teaches it if time allows.

Offering (Group 4): **Group 4 designed a praise banner as an offering of their talents to the Lord.** Group 4 will show and explain the banner. The volunteers will pray and pass the offering containers.

Lord's Supper: God answers prayers! The best example of that is Jesus, God's Son. God heard the prayers of His people asking for a Savior, asking for forgiveness from their sins. God answered those prayers by sending Jesus to earth. When Jesus died on the cross, He died to save us. He died so that our sins could be forgiven. Let's thank God for answering the prayers of many, many people by sending Jesus. Pray and then serve the Lord's Supper.

Scripture (Group 5): **Group 5 has done research on some of the Scriptures that talk about God's hearing and answering prayers. Let's listen to what they found out.** Group 5 shares Scriptures and paraphrases.

Devotion: When we love someone, we like to talk to him. We like to listen to what he says. We like to give him things, especially things he asks for.

Parents are like that. They listen to us, they talk to us, they give us things. They try to give us what we ask for. But sometimes parents say, "No." Sometimes they may say, "You'll have to wait for that." Sometimes they say, "Yes, but you must do this first." Sometimes they give us what we want before we've even asked for it. Sometimes they give us something even better than what we've asked for!

We might not like it when they say, "No," or "Wait." But they have reasons for saying that. Parents know things their children don't know. Parents sometimes can see that giving us what we ask for may actually be bad for us. Or we may need to be older, so we have to wait. Sometimes they have something better planned. We have to trust our parents to do what they think is best for us, even when we don't understand why they answer our requests the way they do.

God loves us very much! He knows everything about us! He even knows what we want or need before we ask for it. But He still wants to hear us talk to Him and ask Him our requests.

Because God knows everything, He knows what is best for us. That is why sometimes He may answer our requests, "No," or "Wait awhile." Sometimes it hurts to wait or we can't understand why God doesn't seem to hear or answer our prayers. But God knows everything and He loves us very much. God does what is best for us, and we must trust Him. We may not understand, but the God who loves us does. He always answers our prayers in a way that is best for us.

Prayer (Group 6): **Group 6 will help us update our prayer chart.** Group 6 updates the chart; then reads the thank-you notes as a closing prayer.

Closing Moments
(10-15 minutes)

Stained-glass picture. Provide copies of Activity Page 4C, crayons, scissors, cotton balls, baby oil, newspaper, and paper towels.

Pupils will color the stained-glass picture on the activity page to reveal the message, "God answers prayer." Then they should cut around the border of the picture. Lay the pictures on newspaper. Use the cotton balls to spread a very thin layer of baby oil on each picture. Lay the pictures on several layers of paper towels for the pupils to take home. At home the children can blot the excess oil and then hang their stained-glass pictures.

Praise Acrostic

Use the letters below to write praise words or phrases to God. Praise Him because He promises to answer our prayers.

G
O
D

A
N
S
W
E
R
S

P
R
A
Y
E
R
S

Does God Listen?

Find each of these Scriptures in your Bible. After you have read each one, write it in your own words. Some words are given to help you get started.

2 Chronicles 7:14—If my people, called by my name, will _____
_____
_____

Job 22:27—When you pray, God _____
_____
_____

Psalm 34:15, 17—God watches those who do _____
_____
_____

Psalm 38:15—I'm waiting for _____
_____

Psalm 120:1—When I am _____
_____
_____

Matthew 7:7,8—Ask and God will _____
_____
_____

1 John 5:14—We can be sure _____
_____

MYSTERY REMINDER

Color all the sections with a round dot red. Color the other sections any colors you wish. When you are finished, you will have a reminder of something important to know.

© 1994 by The STANDARD PUBLISHING COMPANY. Permission is granted to photocopy this page for ministry purposes only—not for resale.

**Unit Two
Leaders Trust God
Scripture Text: Matthew 28:1-10**

Session 5

Jesus Is Alive!

Worship Focus

Worship God because He raised Jesus from the dead.

Transition Time

(10-15 minutes)

Send the pupils in small groups to the rest rooms and drinking fountain. Welcome newcomers and involve everyone in the following activity.

Joy Poster. Have a large piece of butcher paper or some large white poster boards and markers or crayons available. Have the paper (boards) on a wall or spread out on the floor where the pupils can have room to work. They should draw pictures or colorful designs to illustrate joy. Keep the poster displayed throughout the entire worship session.

Launching the Theme

(10 minutes)

What were some of the ways you illustrated joy on our classroom poster? (Allow response.) **What are some things that give you joy?** (Allow response.) **There are many things that cause us to have joy, but there is one thing that should stand out among them all. About 2,000 years ago God's Son, Jesus, was killed. That was sad. But Jesus didn't stay dead. That is joyful! Three days later God raised Jesus from the dead. He was alive! He still is alive today! This gives us joy because we now have the hope of conquering death just as Jesus did. Jesus offers us a way to spend eternity with Him in Heaven. We have this hope because of the fact that Jesus is alive, even after He was killed. Today we will worship God for raising Jesus from the dead.**

Briefly explain the choices of preparation for worship. Allow each pupil to choose the activity in which he or she would like to participate.

Building the Theme

(30 minutes)

1. Call to Worship. For this activity you will need a poster board or chalkboard and Bibles. The pupils will create an acrostic. Write the words *Jesus Is Alive* vertically down the center of the poster board. The pupils are to think of twelve sentences about Jesus' death and resurrection that contain the letters found in the words *Jesus Is Alive.* (For example: **A**rose on the third day; **L**ove is the reason Jesus went to the cross; **I**nto the tomb they put His body, and so on.) During *Sharing in Worship,* pupils will take turns reading their sentences for the Call to Worship.

If your group is large, divide them into several small groups. Have one or two groups work on the facts of Jesus' death, and the others on His resurrection. Use Luke 22:63-65 along with Matthew 27 for Jesus' trials and crucifixion, and Matthew 28:1-10 and Luke 24:1-12 for His resurrection. While the pupils work, focus a discussion on helping them understand the events. **What happened to Jesus when it was decided He should be crucified?** (He was flogged [beaten], had a crown of thorns placed on His head, was mocked, and hung on a cross.) **What happened when Jesus died?** (The temple curtain was torn; the earth shook; tombs broke open, and so on.) **How and where was Jesus buried?** (He was wrapped in a clean cloth and buried in a tomb. A big stone was rolled in front of the entrance.) **What did Mary Magdalene and the other Mary find when they went to Jesus' tomb later?** (Jesus was not in the tomb. They met Jesus while running to the disciples.)

2. Devotion. For this activity provide Bibles, paper, pencils, and simple costumes. The pupils will read the resurrection account found in Matthew 28:1-10 and write a short skit based on the events given here. The pupils should practice the skit to present as the introduction to the Devotion, during *Sharing in Worship.*

What happened when Mary Magdalene and the other Mary went to Jesus' tomb? (An earthquake; an angel rolled away the stone and sat on it; the guards fainted.) **How do you think the women felt?** (Scared, curious.) **What did the angel tell them?** (Jesus was gone, He had risen. They should go tell the disciples that they would see Jesus alive again.) **What occurred next?** (As they ran to tell the disciples, they met Jesus.) **How do you think they felt then?** (Scared, happy, excited, and so on.)

3. Scripture. You will need copies of Activity Page 5A, pencils, and Bibles for this activity. The pupils will write interview questions and replies for Peter, John, and Mary. Choose a pupil to read the interviewer's questions; the rest of the group can take turns responding for Peter, John, and Mary. They will present the interview immediately after the Devotion during *Sharing in Worship.*

As the pupils work, help them think of questions these people may have had at Jesus' resurrection. Stimulate the pupils' thinking by asking questions such as these. **What do you think these people thought about Jesus before He was killed? How do you think they felt when He died? How did they learn about the resurrection? Do you think they believed the news when they heard Jesus was alive? Why do you think God allowed Jesus to die?**

4. Scripture. For this activity, make copies of Activity Page 5B, and have pencils and Bibles ready. The pupils will compose lists of sad and happy events concerning Jesus' death and resurrection, using the Scriptures given on the activity page. They will begin with Jesus' triumphal entry into Jerusalem.

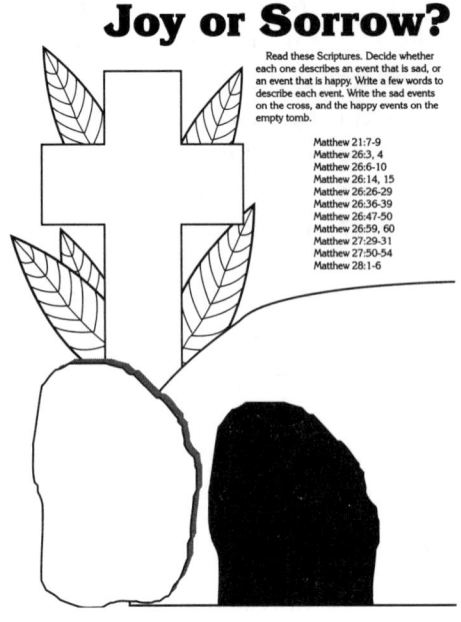

Activity Page 5B

If your group is large, you may want to have the pupils write their lists on poster board, the chalkboard, or on an overhead transparency so everyone can see. Decide on how the group will present the material during *Sharing in Worship* and practice the presentation.

5. Music. Provide paper, pencils, and Bibles for this activity. A musical instrument or tape player would be helpful but is optional. Have the pupils sing the chorus, "He Is Lord." Using that tune, have them write additional stanzas that focus on the resurrection. Use Matthew 28:1-10 for background. The pupils should practice singing the new stanzas to present as special music just before the Lord's Supper, during *Sharing in Worship*. If you think your pupils will need an accompaniment to sing by, have someone prepared to play a musical instrument, or have the song recorded ahead of time.

6. Personal Praise. Provide copies of Activity Page 5C, scissors, glue, markers, and Bible. Have the pupils cut out the cube found on the activity page. Then have them look up the Scriptures given to answer the question, "Why should we worship?" On each side of the cube the pupils will illustrate the verse or draw a way they can worship God. Then they should glue the tabs to form the cubes. Let pupils work alone or with a partner.

During *Sharing in Worship*, have the group stand in front of the large group and take turns reading the Scriptures and then reading their own words or explaining their illustrations. If you want, have each child flip his or her cube onto a table or the floor and then read or tell about the side that is on top.

Sharing in Worship
(20-25 minutes)

Omit any of the following if you did not offer the corresponding activity. The Devotion can be used without the group activity.

Call to Worship (Group 1): **Today we will worship God because He raised Jesus form the dead. Group 1 wrote an acrostic using the words *Jesus Is Alive*.** Have the pupils take turns reading the sentences they wrote.

Devotion (Group 2): **Group 2 has prepared a skit. They will now present the story of the resurrection of Jesus.** After the pupils present the skit, continue with the Devotion.

Imagine how you would have felt after seeing Jesus crucified on the cross. To watch someone you love die a slow and painful death would be a horrible thing! Mary Magdalene and the other Mary had watched Jesus hanging on the cross. They saw Him suffer and die. They were probably very, very sad. They went to Jesus' tomb after the Sabbath, on the first day of the week. Luke tells us that they went to put spices on His body. But a very strange thing happened. There was an earthquake and an angel appeared. The women must have

been frightened. But the angel told them not to be afraid, for Jesus had risen, just as He said He would. The women were told to go tell the disciples that He had risen from the dead. The Bible tells us the women were afraid yet filled with joy. Suddenly Jesus met them! How do you think they felt? (Allow response.) The Bible says they clasped His feet and worshiped Him.

Why does this story give us hope and joy? (Allow response.) Since Jesus rose from the dead we know He is who He said He is—God's Son. And since Jesus is God's Son, we know what He says is true—we will be victorious over death just as He was. We don't have to fear death or what will happen to us. We know we can spend eternity with Jesus in Heaven. Knowing that we have the hope of victory over eternal death gives us joy. Praise God for raising Jesus from the dead!

Scripture (Group 3): **Group 3 had an interview with three of Jesus' friends, Peter, John, and Mary.** Have the pupils present the interview.

Scripture (Group 4): **There were many sad events as well as happy events at the time of Jesus' death and resurrection.** Have the pupils share their information.

Music (Group 5): **Group 5 has written new words to a song about the resurrection of Jesus. Let's listen to them; then they will teach us the words.**

Lord's Supper: We have joy and hope because of Jesus' resurrection. But Jesus first had to suffer and die a painful death on the cross. He chose to do this because of His love for us. As we take the Lord's Supper, let's remember Jesus' choice to die for us.

Offering: God gave His Son for us. One way we can thank Him is by giving our offerings to Him. As we give, let's thank God for His wonderful gift to us. Have a pupil ready to pray for the offering and others to collect it.

Personal Praise (Group 6): **Group 6 did some research on why we should worship God. We know He gave us Jesus, but the Bible also tells us other reasons we should worship Him. Group 6 made cubes illustrating reasons or ways we can worship God.** Have pupils share their cubes at this time.

Closing Moments
(10-15 minutes)

Have the pupils pass a beanbag around a circle while listening to music about Jesus' death and resurrection. Stop the music periodically. Whoever is holding the beanbag should tell a way He will worship God this week.

Write an Interview

Use your imagination to write an interview with some of Jesus' friends. Think of what they might have said about His death and resurrection. Scriptures are given to help you.

Matthew 28:1-10
INTERVIEWER: _____
MARY: _____
INTERVIEWER: _____
MARY: _____

John 20:1-9
INTERVIEWER: _____
PETER: _____
INTERVIEWER: _____
JOHN: _____

Joy or Sorrow?

Read these Scriptures. Decide whether each one describes an event that is sad, or an event that is happy. Write a few words to describe each event. Write the sad events on the cross, and the happy events on the empty tomb.

Matthew 21:7-9
Matthew 26:3, 4
Matthew 26:6-10
Matthew 26:14, 15
Matthew 26:26-29
Matthew 26:36-39
Matthew 26:47-50
Matthew 26:59, 60
Matthew 27:29-31
Matthew 27:50-54
Matthew 28:1-6

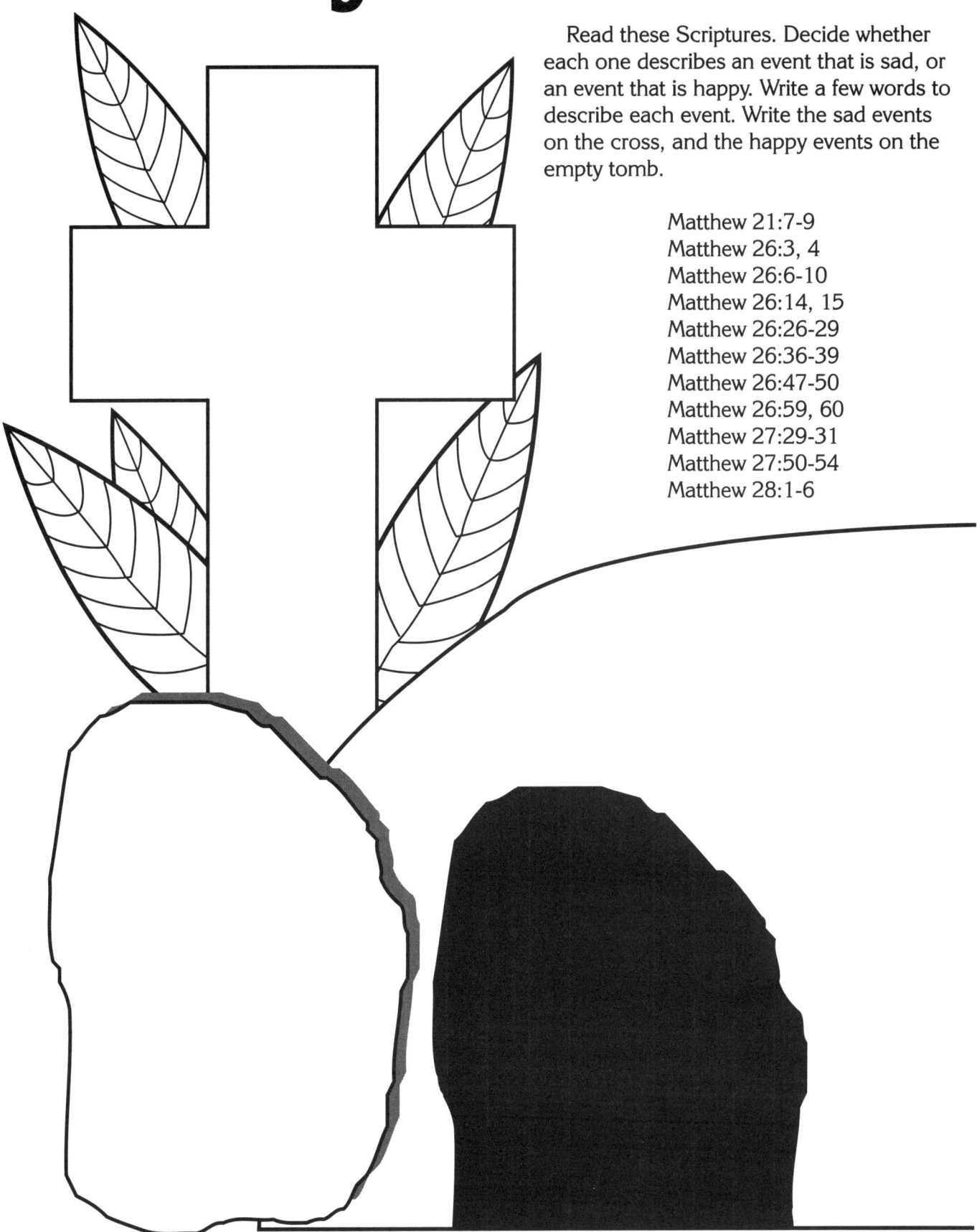

Worship Cube

Why should we worship? Look up the Scriptures on the cube pattern below to find answers to that question. Write a phrase on each side of the cube or draw a picture to illustrate what the verse says. Then cut out the cube on the solid lines, fold on the dotted lines, and glue the tabs in place.

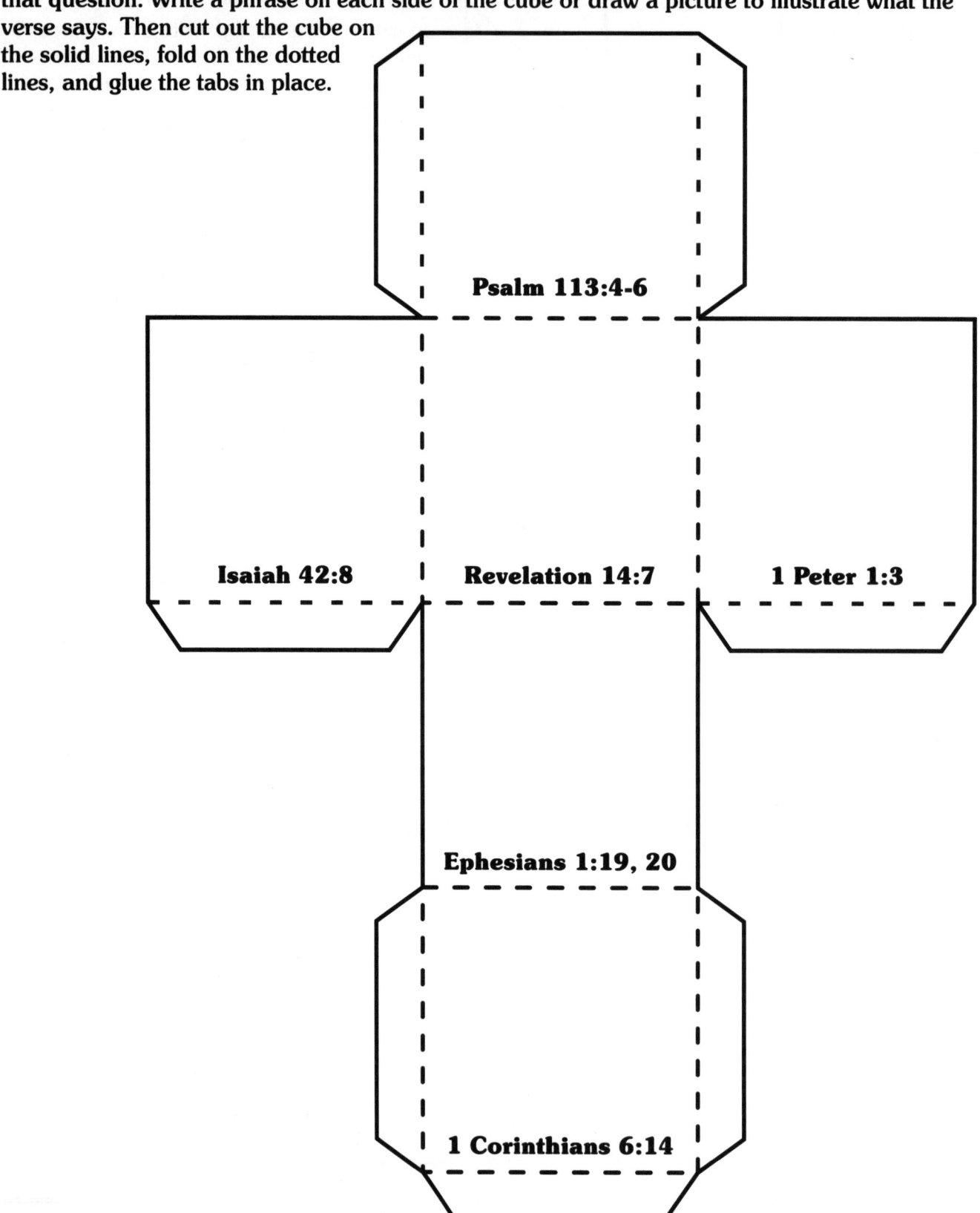

Psalm 113:4-6

Isaiah 42:8   Revelation 14:7   1 Peter 1:3

Ephesians 1:19, 20

1 Corinthians 6:14

5C © 1994 by The STANDARD PUBLISHING COMPANY. Permission is granted to photocopy this page for ministry purposes only—not for resale.

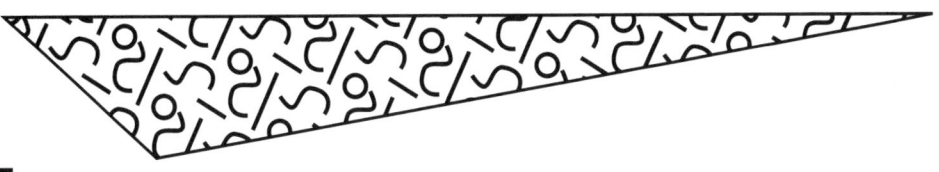

Unit Two
Leaders Trust God
Scripture Text: Judges 6:1, 6, 12-16; 7:2-4, 6-8, 16, 19-21

Session 6

With God, Nothing Is Impossible

Worship Focus

Worship God because He helps us.

Transition Time

(10-15 minutes)

Send the pupils in small groups to the rest rooms and drinking fountain. Welcome newcomers and involve everyone in the following activity.

Wrong Order. Before class write the following verse on strips of paper, putting one word on each strip: "We wait in hope for the Lord; he is our help and our shield," (Psalm 33:20). Hide the strips of paper throughout the room. As the pupils enter, tell them there are fifteen strips of paper, with special words written on them, hidden in the room. The pupils need to find all the words and put the verse in the correct order.

If you have a large class, make two sets of papers, using two colors of paper. Divide the children into two teams, tell them what color of paper to look for, and let them have a little friendly competition as they hunt and put the words in order.

Launching the Theme

(10 minutes)

Were you able to figure out the correct order of the verse? Who can tell me the verse? (Allow a pupil to say the verse aloud.) **What does this verse tell us about our Lord?** (He is our help and shield.) **What does a shield do?** (Protects.) **How does this verse make you feel?** (Allow pupils to respond.) **We know that God is always with us and will help us and protect us. When are some times when you need God's help?** (Allow response.) **We are never alone. God is always there to help us in whatever situation we may be. Today we are worshiping God because He helps us.**

Briefly explain the choices of preparation for worship. Allow the pupils to choose the groups in which they would like to participate.

Building the Theme

(30 minutes)

1. Call to Worship. This could be a challenge activity. You will need copies of Activity Page 6A, pencils, and Bibles. Have the pupils write a responsive reading using the verses from psalms that are printed on the activity page. The reading will tell about God's help to us. During *Sharing in Worship,* the entire group can participate in the reading. Group 1 will read the leader's part and the rest of the large group will say the words, "God is our refuge and strength, an ever-present help in trouble." You may want to have these words written on a chalkboard, poster board, or on an overhead transparency for the entire group to see.

Focus a discussion on helping the pupils find ways God helps us. **How do we see God helping us in Psalm 3?** (He is a shield; He lifts my head; He sustains me; He delivers me.) **In Psalm 9?** (The Lord is a refuge for the oppressed, a stronghold in times of trouble.) **In Psalm 16?** (He counsels me; He is at my right hand.) **In Psalm 18?** (He is my strength, rock, fortress, deliverer.)

2. Devotion. For this activity you will need Bibles, markers or crayons, and a roll of newsprint or butcher paper. Have the pupils read the account of Gideon in the lesson text from Judges. Then have them create a mural illustrating the events in chronological order.

As the pupils work, focus a discussion to help them understand the events. **Why were the Israelites in the hands of the Midianites?** (The Israelites were doing evil; they were worshiping false gods.) **What did an angel tell Gideon?** (God was with him; he would save Israel from the Midianites.) **What was Gideon's reaction to this?** (He said he was weak and didn't know how he could possibly defeat the Midianites.) **What did God tell him?** (He would help Gideon.) **When Gideon gathered an army together, what did God say was wrong?** (Too many men; the Israelites would think they had defeated the Midianites all by themselves.) **How did God say to get rid of the excess army?** (Send home all who were afraid; choose those who lapped the water from their hands.) **What happened?** (The Israelites overcame the Midianites by God's help.)

3. Scripture. For this activity you will need copies of Activity Page 6B, pencils, newsprint, markers, and Bibles. Have the pupils read the Scripture text for today from Judges. The group will work together to create either a word search puzzle or crossword puzzle. Have a volunteer make a large copy of the puzzle on newsprint to be worked by the class during *Sharing in Worship.* The pupils should use words from the verses listed on the activity page. As the pupils work, focus a discussion on the events of the story.

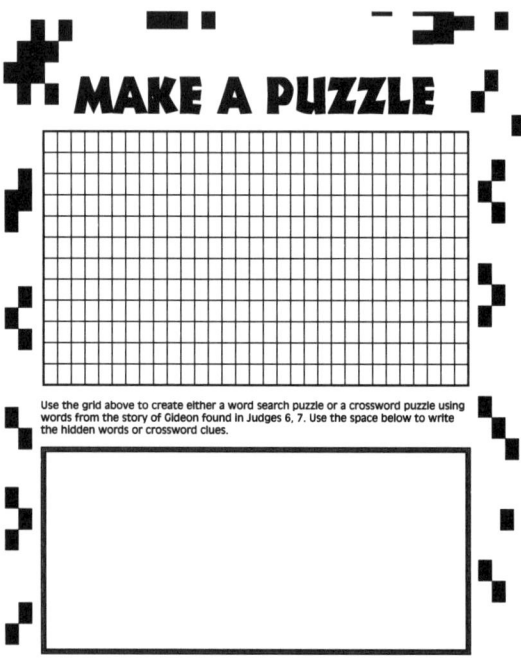

Activity Page 6B

4. Scripture. For this activity you will need copies of Activity Page 6C, pencils, and Bibles. Have the pupils read Psalm 25. They should look for ways that God helps them. They can illustrate these verses; then cut them out and staple them together to form a book. During *Sharing in Worship,* have pupils split up and show their books to individuals or small groups of pupils.

What does Psalm 25 tell us about God's help? (He is our Savior; He instructs sinners; He guides and teaches the humble; He will free us from anguish; He takes away our sins; He will guard and rescue us; He will protect us.)

5. Personal Praise. Have ready poster board, markers, magazines, scissors, and glue. The pupils should think of specific situations in their lives when God has helped them. Then they will construct collages illustrating these times. During *Sharing in Worship,* pupils will take turns showing their collages and explaining them. Have them say something like this: "When I was at school, God helped me by _____. Praise God for helping me!"

When have you needed God's help at school? (Allow response.) **What things do you need that God helps you to have? When you are with friends, what kind of help can God give you? How does God help you when you are alone?**

6. Prayer. For this activity you will need construction paper (cut into strips, about 2" x 9"), pens, markers, scissors, and clear, self-adhesive plastic. These pupils will make bookmarks. Pupils should write a short prayer to God, thanking Him for a specific time He helped him or her. Pupils may write their prayers on one side and decorate the other side of the bookmarks. Then help them cover both sides of the bookmarks with the clear, self-adhesive plastic. Group 6 will read their prayers to begin the large group prayer time at the close of *Sharing in Worship.*

When are times God helps us? (Allow response.) **God is always with us and is always aware of times when we need His help. He always knows exactly the best way to help us, in whatever situation we may be. Whether we need strength, courage, comfort, a listener, or a physical need, God is able to help us. Many times He helps us through other people, such as parents, grandparents, teachers, Christian friends, and so forth.**

Sharing in Worship
(20-25 minutes)

Omit any of the following if you did not offer the corresponding activity. The Devotion can be used without the group activity.

Call to Worship (Group 1): **Group 1 wrote a responsive reading telling about God's help to us. They used verses from the book of Psalms that tell about God's help.** Have the group teach the others their sentence to say—"God is our refuge and strength, an ever-present help in trouble." Then have everyone participate in the responsive reading.

Devotion (Group 2): **Group 2 prepared a mural to illustrate our Devotion.** Have the group hold up the mural and briefly explain the illustrations. Then continue with the Devotion.

The Israelites still had not learned their lesson. They chose, once again, to worship false gods. So God gave them into the hands of the Midianites. Because of the cruelty of the Midianites, the Israelites hid in caves and mountain clefts for seven years. They cried to God for help. God sent an angel to talk to Gideon. The angel told Gideon he would save the Israelites. Gideon knew he was a weak man, but God promised to help him.

God wanted the Israelites to understand that it was His power

helping them, not theirs, that would defeat the Midianites. God helped Gideon reduce the number of his army to three hundred men, and, with God's help, the Israelites were successful.

In this story about Gideon, we can see how God helped a very few men to accomplish His work. And God will help you too. When you feel you are too weak or scared to do something God wants you to do, remember the story of Gideon. Remember the words found in Philippians 4 13: "I can do everything through him who gives me strength."

Scripture (Group 3): **Group 3 made a puzzle containing words from Judges 6 and 7.** Have the entire class participate in solving the large unfinished copy of the puzzle. Group 3 pupils can give clues when the other pupils seem to need help.

Scripture (Group 4): **Group 4 did a study of Psalm 25 and found ways God helps us. They are going to show you the books they made using this information.**

Lord's Supper: Today, we've learned that God helps us in many ways. He knew we needed a Savior. He knew we needed help to be able to have our sins forgiven. God helped us by sending His Son, Jesus, to earth to die for us. Because God helped us in this way, our sins are forgiven and we know we can spend eternity with Him in Heaven. Let's remember this as we take the Lord's Supper.

Offering: God helps us in so many ways. We have an opportunity to help others by the giving of our offerings. When we give to God we are saying, "Thank You for helping us."

Personal Praise (Group 5): **Group 5 created collages showing times when God helped them.** Have the group members show their collages.

Prayer (Group 6): Have the pupils form a prayer circle. **Group 6 wrote prayers to God thanking Him for specific times He helped them. Let's think of times when God helped us.** After a couple of minutes, Group 6 will read their prayers. Then anyone who wishes to pray aloud may do so.

Closing Moments
(10-15 minutes)

Have a short praise time of singing. Have the pupils try to think of songs or choruses they know that tell about God's help. Some possibilities are: "Reach Out to Jesus," "God Will Take Care of You," What a Friend We Have in Jesus." If there is time, add stanzas to "God Is So Good." (For example: God has helped me; God answers prayer; God gives me strength.)

Praise God!

Read verses from the book of Psalms to find out ways God helps us. Write a responsive reading that your group can lead.

All: God is our refuge and strength, an ever-present help in trouble.

Solo 1 (Psalm 3:3, 4): _____
_____
_____

All (Psalm 46:1): _____

Duet (Psalm 9:9, 10): _____
_____
_____

All (Psalm 46:1): _____

Solo 2 (Psalm 16:7, 8): _____
_____
_____

All (Psalm 46:1): _____

Solo 1 (Psalm 18:2, 3): _____
_____
_____

All (Psalm 46:1): _____
_____

MAKE A PUZZLE

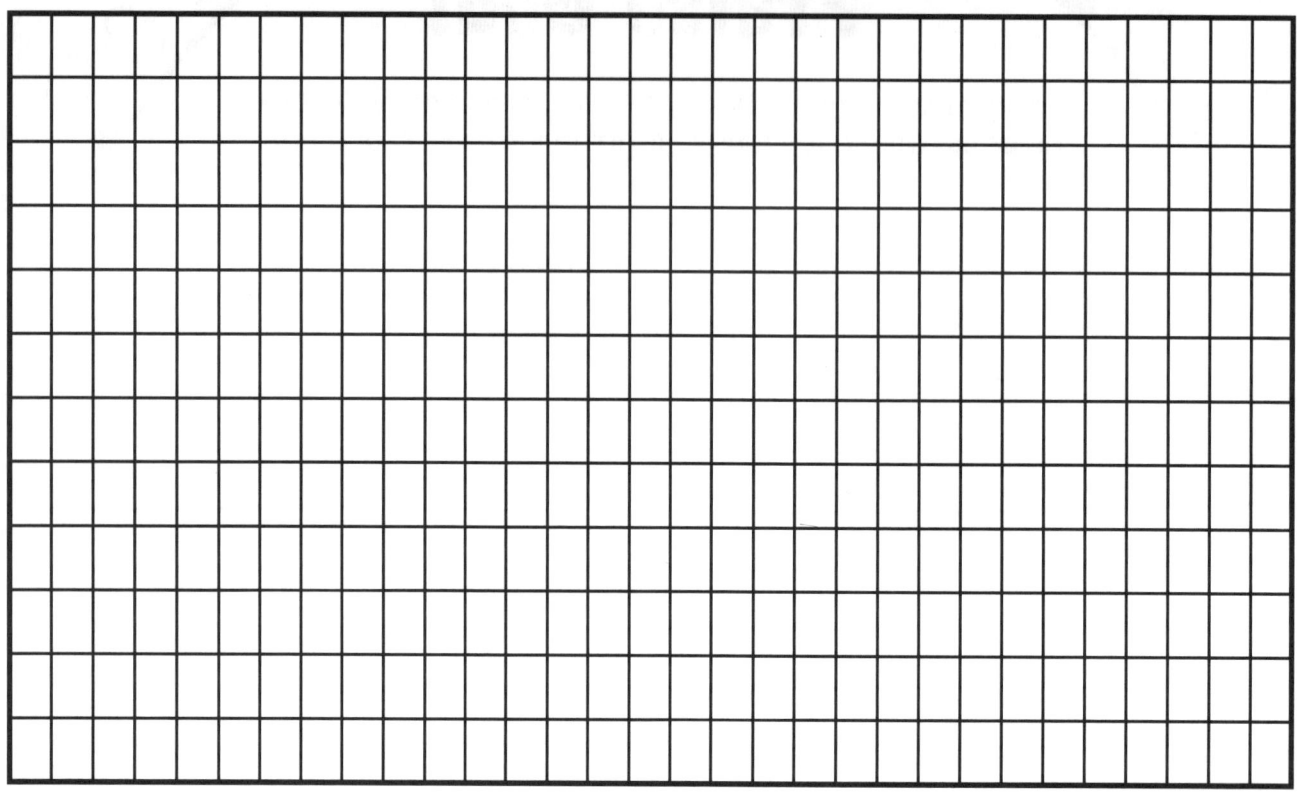

Use the grid above to create either a word search puzzle or a crossword puzzle using words from the story of Gideon found in Judges 6, 7. Use the space below to write the hidden words or crossword clues.

Make a "God Helps Me" Book

Read Psalm 25 to find ways God helps you. In each of the boxes below, write one way God helps you. Then cut on the solid lines, fold on the dotted line, and staple the pages together to form a book.

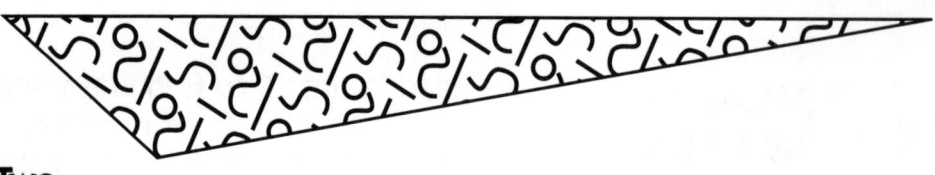

Unit Two
Leaders Trust God
Scripture Text: Judges 13:1; 15:20; 16:4-6, 16-19, 21-23, 25-30

Session 7

The World's Strongest Man Becomes Weak

Worship Focus

Worship God because He gives us strength.

Transition Time
(10-15 minutes)

Send pupils in small groups to the rest rooms and drinking fountain. Welcome newcomers and involve everyone in the following activity.

How Strong Are You? Before class, write on separate slips of paper various jobs for the pupils to do. Have some easy jobs, such as sharpening a pencil or throwing away a piece of paper. Have some jobs that will require a lot of strength, such as lifting a heavy pile of books or moving a file cabinet. Let the pupils take turns choosing a slip of paper and then doing the job listed.

Launching the Theme
(10 minutes)

Who was not able to do the job listed on his piece of paper? Why were you not able to complete it? (Allow response.) Some of the jobs were simple, others required a lot of strength. What are some things that give you strength? (Allow response.) **If we believe advertisements we see and hear, we would believe we can get strength from things such as vitamins, certain foods, exercise, good health, proper rest, the right pair of shoes, and so on. While it may be true that some of these things help us to have physical strength, only God is always able to give us the strength we need, just when we need it. Whether it be physical strength, emotional strength, or spiritual strength, God is able to provide it for us at just the right time. Today we will worship God because He gives us strength.**

Briefly explain the choices of preparation for worship. Allow the pupils to choose the groups in which they would like to participate.

50

Building the Theme

(30 minutes)

1. Call to Worship. For this activity you will need Bibles, a large piece of felt or other stiff fabric, scraps of fabric from which you can cut out letters, glue, scissors, glitter, sequins, yarn. Have the pupils look up Isaiah 40:31. Then have them construct a banner using a portion of that verse; for example, "Those who hope in the Lord will renew their strength." Have pupils decorate the banner with the various art supplies.

As the pupils work, talk about the verse. **What will God do for those who hope in Him?** (Renew their strength.) **What does it mean to "soar on wings like eagles"?** (Allow response.) **What two things will we be able to do when the Lord renews our strength?** (Run and not grow weary; walk and not be faint.)

For the Call to Worship, have two pupils hold up the banner while one pupil reads the Scripture. Then have all of Group 1 say in unison, "Praise God because He gives us strength."

2. Devotion. For this activity provide a shoe box for each pupil, construction paper and markers, glue, scissors, and Bibles. Have the pupils read the story of Samson found in Judges. Have the lesson Scripture references printed on a chalkboard or a poster board. Group 2 will create diorama scenes to illustrate the story. During the Devotion, they will show their dioramas in chronological order, as an adult speaks. If your group is large, have pupils work in pairs.

As the pupils work, help them to understand the events that occurred. **Why was Samson's hair not to be cut?** (Samson had been dedicated to God from birth. Not cutting his hair was one provision of his dedication.) **What important thing was Samson going to do?** (Begin the deliverance of Israel from the Philistines.) **What was the name of the woman Samson fell in love with?** (Delilah.) **How did Delilah agree to help the Philistines?** (Find out Samson's great strength so the Philistines could subdue [capture] him.) **Did Delilah find the secret of Samson's strength?** (Yes, he finally gave in and told her that his hair couldn't be cut.) **What happened when the secret was discovered?** (Samson's hair was cut and he was taken prisoner. They bound him with shackles and poked his eyes out.) **How was Samson finally victorious?** (There was a celebration worshiping a false god and the people wanted to see Samson and mock him. As his hair had begun to grow, his strength had returned. With God's help he pushed over some pillars and the temple crashed down, killing about 3,000 Philistines as well as Samson.)

3. Scripture. For this activity you will need copies of Activity Page 7A, Bibles, and pencils. Have the pupils decode the verses about God's strength. They may check their answers in their Bibles. Group 3 will take turns reading the decoded Scriptures just after the Devotion.

Focus a discussion on helping the pupils understand what God's Word says about God's strength. **Who is our strength?** (God.) **How can we have strength from God?** (If we hope in Him; by seeking His face.) **What does it mean to "seek his face"?** (Pray to Him; read His Word.) **What does God's strength allow us to do?** (We can do everything through Him.) **Does that mean God will help us to do anything we want to do?** (No. He will help us do the things we ought to do.) **What other words are used to describe God's strength?** (He is my song; the joy of the Lord is my strength; He is my shield; He is my refuge and my help in trouble.)

4. Scripture. This could be a challenge activity. Provide copies of Activity Page

7B, Bibles, and pencils. Have the pupils look up the verses given for each Bible character to discover how God gave strength to that person. Then pupils will write short summaries of what they have read. During *Sharing in Worship,* pupils will take turns reading their statements about these Bible people after Group 3 reads their decoded verses.

What are some ways God provided strength to these people? (He provided them with food and water; with strength to do what was right; He gave them courage when they were in frightening situations, and so on.)

5. Personal Praise. This also could be a challenge activity. You will need paper and pencils for this activity. Have the pupils write three stories about God providing strength. Divide the group into three small groups. Have one group work on a story about God providing physical strength, one on His providing emotional strength, and one spiritual strength. Have pupils end their stories with a statement of praise or thanks to God for His strength. The pupils will take turns reading their stories aloud just after the Offering during *Sharing in Worship.*

Before writing, discuss the differences of these areas. **When are times you may need physical strength from God?** (Allow response. When you are sick or tired or hurt.) **When do you need emotional strength?** (When you are going through a hard time, such as a death or maybe someone treats you unfairly, and so on.) **When do you need spiritual strength?** (When you are doubting or feeling far from God, and so on.) **How do you get that strength?** (Prayer, reading the Bible, coming to Sunday school and worship, talking to a Christian friend.)

6. Prayer. Provide an assortment of greeting cards (with or without messages), pens, paper, postage stamps, and Bibles. Also have a list of names and addresses of people who would appreciate hearing from your pupils. Pupils will compose a short note to include in the cards. Make sure a verse of Scripture is included in the message. Write this on a chalkboard or poster board as they decide what to say. Then have some pupils copy the note on paper or inside the cards while the others address and stamp the envelopes. **Option:** Provide construction paper, markers, glue, scissors, envelopes, and stamps. Let pupils make their own cards to send.

Do you know someone in need of God's strength—someone who is sick, or is going through hard times? (Allow pupils to respond.) **How do you think that person would feel if he or she were reminded of God's strength?** (Allow response.) **I have a list of some people from our congregation who would certainly appreciate getting cards from you. We are going to send cards that will encourage these people. Then we are going to get ready to pray for them.** After the cards are completed, ask for volunteers who will pray for these people at the close of *Sharing in Worship.* In order to make the prayers more specific, you may want to discuss the particular needs of these people as pupils work.

Sharing in Worship
(20-25 minutes)

Omit any of the following if you did not include the corresponding activity. The Devotion can be used without the group activity.

Call to Worship (Group 1): **Group 1 created a banner telling about God's strength.** Have the group display the banner and explain it to the others. They will finish by saying in unison, "Praise God because He gives us strength."

Devotion (Group 2): Have pupils in Group 2 share their dioramas in chronological order. Keep them displayed during the Devotion.

God allowed the Philistines to rule over the Israelites for forty years because the Israelites had disobeyed God again. God chose Samson to be the deliverer. How do you think Samson's parents felt when the angel told them they would have a son to be set apart for God's use? (Allow response.)

When Samson grew to be a man he fell in love with a woman named Delilah, who wanted to know the secret of his power. She planned to tell the Philistines, who would pay her well. Samson finally told her that if his hair were to be cut, he would become weak. As a result, his hair was cut and he was taken prisoner. He was bound and blinded.

God, however, once more provided strength for Samson. At a celebration of the Philistines, Samson knocked down two pillars and the temple collapsed, killing about 3,000 Philistines and Samson himself.

Did God provide strength for Samson when he needed it? (Yes.) Will God provide strength for us when we need it? (Yes.) Although we won't be in a position similar to Samson's, we will go through times when we need strength—physical, emotional, and spiritual strength. God gives us the strength we need when we need it. Having people pray for us gives us strength. Reading God's Word gives us strength. Having Christian friends gives us strength. Just as God knew exactly the kind of strength Samson needed, He will provide the strength we need.

Scripture (Group 3): **Group 3 decoded verses about God's strength.** Have the pupils take turns saying the verses.

Scripture (Group 4): **Group 4 did some research about other people in the Bible who received strength from God.** Have the pupils share their sentences about these Bible people.

Lord's Supper: We have seen how God provided strength for people in the Bible. We know God provides strength for us as well. God provides many things for us because He loves us. His love for us is why He sent His Son, Jesus, to die for us. As we take the Lord's Supper, let's remember how God provides for us because He loves us.

Offering: As we give our offerings today, let us do so with an attitude of thanks to God for giving us strength.

Personal Praise (Group 5): **Group 5 wrote stories about how God provides different kinds of strength to people.** Have the pupils take turns reading the stories.

Prayer (Group 6): **The pupils in Group 6 prepared (made) cards to send to people to remind them of God's strength.** Have the pupils show their cards to everyone. Have the volunteers pray for the people who will receive the cards. Then close by thanking God for giving us strength.

Closing Moments
(10-15 minutes)

Tic-tac-toe. Divide the pupils into two teams, the "X" team and "O" team. Take turns asking each team a question from today's Bible story about Samson. If the team answers correctly they may place an X or an O on a tic-tac-toe grid drawn on poster board or the chalkboard. If the question is not answered correctly, the other team gets a chance to answer. The first team to get three X's or O's in a line wins. Encourage all the pupils to answer rather than have one or two who are more aggressive or outgoing answer all the questions.

Find the Strength

Decode the following statements to find what the Bible says about God's strength

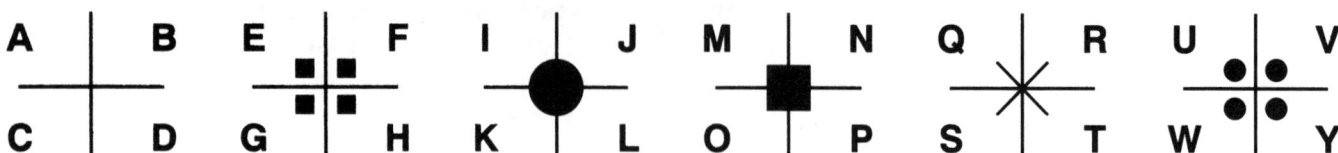

Exodus 15:2 - - The _LORD_ is my _STRENGTH_ and my _SONG_

1 Chronicles 16:11 - - _LOOK_ to the _LORD_ and his strength; _SEEK_ His _FACE_ always.

Nehemiah 8:10b - - For the _JOY_ of the _LORD_ is your _STRENGTH_.

Isaiah 40:31 - - But those who _HOPE_ in the Lord will _RENEW_ their strength.

Philippians 4:13 - - I can do _EVERYTHING_ through _HIM_ who gives me strength.

Psalm 46:1 - - God is our _REFUGE_ and strength, a very present _HELP_ in _TROUBLE_.

7A   © 1994 by The STANDARD PUBLISHING COMPANY. Permission is granted to photocopy this page for ministry purposes only—not for resale.

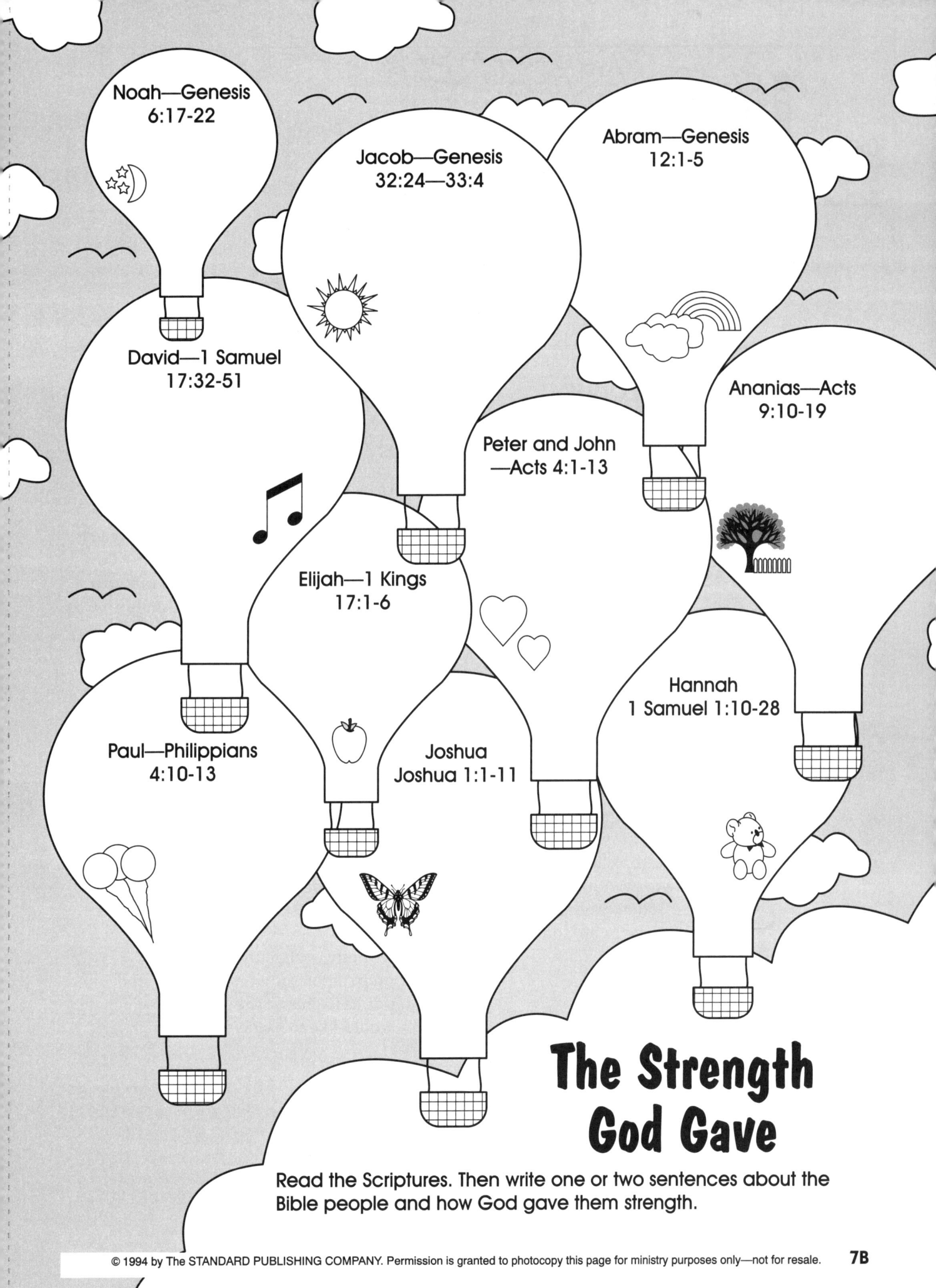

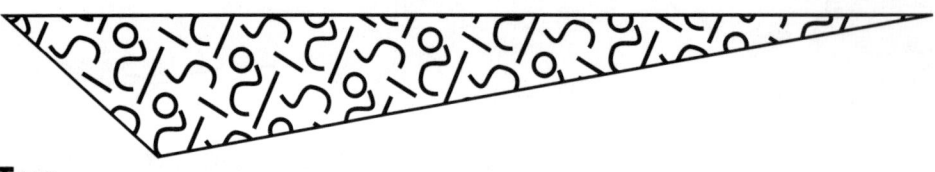

Unit Two
Leaders Trust God
Scripture Text: 1 Samuel 3:1-10, 19, 20

Session 8

God Speaks: We Listen

Worship Focus

Worship God because He speaks to us through His Word.

Transition Time
(10-15 minutes)

Send the pupils in small groups to the rest rooms and drinking fountain. Welcome newcomers and involve everyone in the following activity.

Follow the Directions: Provide each person with a piece of paper and a pencil. Give directions how to draw a house or a cat or some other simple object. (Draw the object ahead of time yourself.) You may only use your voice. After you have completed the directions, compare the pupils' drawings with each others' and with yours. You may be surprised at how some of the pictures turn out!

Launching the Theme
(10 minutes)

How many of you followed my directions and drew something you recognized? (Allow response.) **Why is it important to follow directions?** (Allow response.) **Directions help us to know what to do. What kinds of things give us directions?** (Maps, cookbooks, car manuals, model instructions, and so on.) **What could happen if we didn't have directions?** (We might not know how to get somewhere or how to make something.) **Where do we find directions for living our lives?** (In God's Word.) **God knows what is best for us. He knows we need guidance and direction for our lives. He gives us this information through His Word, the Bible. Today we will worship God because He speaks to us through His Word.**

Briefly explain the choices of preparation for worship. Allow the pupils to choose the groups in which they would like to participate.

56

Building the Theme

● ● ● ● ● ● ● ● ● ● ● ● ● ● ● ● ● ● ●

(30 minutes)

1. Call to Worship. For this activity you will need copies of Activity Page 8A and pencils. Have the pupils write story endings to the situations given on the activity page. The stories should show how someone trusted in God's Word. These stories will be read as the Call to Worship. Let pupils work individually or in pairs. If time is short, assign each story to a pupil or pair of pupils.

Think of some promises God gives to us in His Word that would help in these situations. (God will provide our needs; God is always with us; God always keeps His promises; God provided Jesus so we could go to Heaven, and so on.)

2. Scripture. You will need copies of Activity Page 8B, pencils, and Bibles for this activity. Have the pupils look up the verses listed to find things God says to us in His Word and put them in the proper columns. Pupils will read or tell about their verses right after the Call to Worship.

Look up these verses to find out some of the things God has to say to you. Choose the appropriate column, and then write a few words to summarize the verse. One has been done for you.

Verses	a promise from God's Word	Instructions from God's Word	description from God's Word
Romans 8:1			
Romans 8:18			
Romans 8:28			
Romans 10:9			
Romans 12:1, 2			
Galatians 6:2			
Galatians 6:9, 10			
Ephesians 4:29			
Ephesians 5:19, 20			
Ephesians 6:1, 2		Obey your parents in the Lord	
Ephesians 6:10			
Philippians 4:13			
2 Timothy 3:16, 17			
Titus 3:1, 2			
Hebrews 4:12, 13			

Activity Page 8B

What are some promises God tells us? (No condemnation for those in Christ Jesus; our present sufferings not comparable to later glory; all things work together for good to those who love God, and so on.) **What are some instructions God gives us?** (To be a living sacrifice; carry others' burdens; do good to others, and so on.) **What does God say about His Word?** (It is living and active; it judges thoughts and attitudes of the heart; it is God-breathed and useful for teaching, rebuking, correcting and training in righteousness.)

3. Devotion. This could be a challenge activity. Provide poster board, paper, markers, and Bibles. Have the pupils read 1 Samuel 3:1-10, 19, 20. Then have them write a poem telling about the events of the story. They may use the paper to work and then write the completed poem on the poster board to be read during *Sharing in Worship.* The pupils may illustrate the poem if time permits.

Help the children understand the events. **Who did the boy Samuel think was calling him in the night?** (Eli.) **After three times, what did Eli tell Samuel?** (That the voice was God speaking, and to reply, "Speak, Lord, for your servant is listening.") **What happened as Samuel grew up?** (God was with him. Samuel became a prophet of God.)

4. Scripture. This could be a challenge activity. You will need Bibles, paper, pencils, and a few books about sheep and shepherds (check with your public library for these). Have the pupils read John 10:1-18 about the shepherd and His flock. Then have the pupils do a bit of research on sheep and how they respond to the shepherd, particularly his voice. Divide the group in two. One group will write about sheep and shepherds; the other group will concentrate on our relationship to Jesus, our shepherd. Decide on several parallels and then let the groups write about them. During *Sharing in Worship,* have the group who wrote about sheep and shepherds make a statement, then those who wrote about us and Jesus read their corresponding statement. Continue in this way until they have finished.

Why do sheep follow the shepherd? (They know his voice.) **How do we hear Jesus' voice speak to us?** (Through His Word.) **How does a shepherd care for his sheep? How does Jesus care for us?**

5. Personal Praise. For this activity you will need hangers, yarn or string, a paper punch, tape, markers, and construction paper. Have the pupils think of various ways they can hear God's Word. They will construct a mobile showing these ways. Choose someone to hold up the mobile where everyone can see it during *Sharing in Worship,* right after the Offering. Have the others in Group 5 take turns explaining the symbols on the mobiles. If your group is very large, make several mobiles.

What are some ways God speaks to us? (Through reading the Bible, listening to tapes, watching Christian videos, through people, sermons, missionaries, music, and so on.)

6. Prayer. For this activity provide copies of Activity Page 8C, pencils, and Bibles. Have the pupils choose Bible books they would like to read. Have them use the calendar from the activity page to make a schedule of how much they will read each day.

Choose a book from the Bible you will focus on. Divide the book into verses or chapters and schedule in what you will read each day. It is important to read God's Word daily. Try to stick to your schedule. After you "force" yourself to read daily for awhile, it should become a habit.

Make sure you have a copy of the activity page for each member of the large group. Have Group 6 members pass these out at the close of worship and encourage everyone to fill in the chart and follow it this week. You might want to follow up next week to see how your pupils are doing on their reading. Give them plenty of encouragement on this project.

Sharing in Worship
(20-25 minutes)

Omit any of the following if you did not offer the corresponding activity. The Devotion can be used without the group activity.

Call to Worship (Group 1): **Today we are here to worship God because He speaks to us through His Word. Group 1 wrote some story endings about people who trusted in God's Word.** Have the pupils share their stories. Then have a brief prayer praising and thanking God for His Word.

Scripture (Group 2): **Group 2 found a variety of things God tells us in His Word. We have some directions, encouragement, promises, and others.** Have pupils tell about or read their verses.

Devotion (Group 3): **Group 3 has written a poem to share with us.** Have pupils read their poem aloud. Also display any illustrations. Then continue with the Devotion.

When the boy Samuel heard a voice calling him, he thought it was Eli. But Eli figured out it was God talking to Samuel. He told Samuel to tell God, "Speak, for your servant is listening." God then told Samuel that Eli's family was going to be punished for their many sins. Imagine how Samuel must have felt when Eli wanted to know what God had told Samuel! But Eli responded by saying, "He is the Lord; let him do what is good in his eyes." He realized that

God knew what was best. Samuel continued to grow and people knew he was a prophet of the Lord. God continued to reveal himself to Samuel through His word.

Does God have anything to say to us today? (Allow response.) **Yes! God loves us so very much and wants us to have guidance and direction in our lives so we will do what He knows is best for us. God gave us His Word, the Bible, so we would know what He has to say to us. He gives us directions, promises, encouragement, hope, reasons to live, examples to follow, and much more! God does speak to us today, just as He spoke to Samuel so long ago. All we have to do is listen, or pick up our Bibles and read. If we can say with Samuel, "Speak, Lord, your servant is listening," God will have plenty to say to us.**

Scripture (Group 4): **Group 4 has done some research on sheep and shepherds. Listen carefully to see how we are like sheep.**

Lord's Supper: **God loves us so much He gave us His Word so we could know what He wants to tell us. Just as sheep hear the caring voice of their shepherd, we, too, can listen to our shepherd, Jesus. As we take the Lord's Supper, let's think about Jesus, our shepherd, who loved us so much He chose to die for us.**

Offering: **One of God's instructions to us in His Word is to give freely. As we give our offerings, let's be thankful God cares enough about us to speak to us through His Word.**

Personal Praise (Group 5): **Group 5 made mobiles showing us the many ways we have available to learn from God's Word.** Have the pupils share their mobiles.

Prayer (Group 6): **God speaks to us through His Word. But we must read it to find out what He wants us to know. Group 6 has created individual schedules to help them be consistent in their Bible reading.** Have pupils share. After the designated pupils have handed out the blank schedules, close in group prayer, asking God to help pupils follow their Bible reading schedules.

Closing Moments
(10-15 minutes)

Reading Reminders. Provide poster board, cut into fourths, or construction paper; crayons or markers; paper punch and yarn to make hangers (optional). Have pupils make posters to take home to remind them to read God's Word regularly. Remind pupils to hang the posters where they will see them daily.

FINISH THE STORY

Write endings for these situations. Your story should show how the girl or boy involved trusted in God's Word.

Monica's parents were getting divorced. She was sad and worried about what would happen to her family.

Danny was afraid he could never be good enough to get into Heaven.

Ali's dad lost his job. She overheard her parents talking about not having enough money to pay the bills.

Marcus is going alone to visit his grandmother. He's going to fly on a plane without his parents and he's never flown before.

Alex had to change schools in the middle of the year because his family moved. He didn't know a single person at his new school.

Sonya's friends laughed at her and told her she was stupid for going to church.

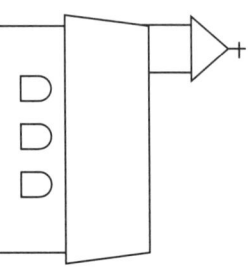

8A © 1994 by The STANDARD PUBLISHING COMPANY. Permission is granted to photocopy this page for ministry purposes only—not for resale.

Look up these verses to find out some of the things God has to say to you. Choose the appropriate column, and then write a few words to summarize the verse. One has been done for you.

Verses	a promise from God's Word	instructions from God's Word	description from God's Word
Romans 8:1			
Romans 8:18			
Romans 8:28			
Romans 10:9			
Romans 12:1, 2			
Galatians 6:2			
Galatians 6:9, 10			
Ephesians 4:29			
Ephesians 5:19, 20			
Ephesians 6:1, 2		Obey your parents in the Lord	
Ephesians 6:10			
Philippians 4:13			
2 Timothy 3:16, 17			
Titus 3:1, 2			
Hebrews 4:12, 13			

© 1994 by The STANDARD PUBLISHING COMPANY. Permission is granted to photocopy this page for ministry purposes only—not for resale.

Schedule Your Scripture Reading

Month _____   Year _____

SUNDAY	MONDAY	TUESDAY	WEDNESDAY	THURSDAY	FRIDAY	SATURDAY

Choose one book of the Bible to read. Then fill in the calendar, scheduling how you'll read the book you've chosen. You may want to do a few verses each day, or a chapter. You decide. Your responsibility is to stick to the schedule so you read something each day from God's Word.

© 1994 by The STANDARD PUBLISHING COMPANY. Permission is granted to photocopy this page for ministry purposes only—not for resale.

**Unit Two
Leaders Trust God
Scripture Text:** 1 Samuel 8:4, 5, 21, 22; 9:15-17;
10:1, 17-19, 21, 23, 24

Session 9

Be Good Followers

Worship Focus

Worship God because He helps us to follow leaders.

Transition Time

(10-15 minutes)

Send the pupils in small groups to the rest rooms and drinking fountain. Welcome newcomers and involve everyone in the following activity.

Name That Leader! Allow pupils to play individually or divide the group into two teams. Give each pupil (team) a piece of paper and a pencil. Set a timer for three minutes. During the three minutes have pupils (or teams) compose a list of leaders or authority figures in their lives. When time is up, see which pupil or team has the longest list. Then compose one large list of leaders using what the pupils have written.

Launching the Theme

(10 minutes)

Display the list from the previous activity. **How many of you were aware of the number of leaders in your life? What would happen if we had no leaders or authority figures in our lives?** (Allow response.) **Our world would probably be total chaos. Everyone would do what he or she wanted to do and people would get hurt or killed. Are leaders and laws important?** (Allow response.) **Do you think God thinks leaders and laws are important? God's Word tells us that we are to obey our leaders and submit to their authority. This isn't always easy, but God loves us and knows what is best for us. If God tells us to obey our leaders, we should do it. It is for our own good. Today we are worshiping God because He helps us to follow leaders.**

Briefly explain the choices of preparation for worship. Allow the pupils to choose the groups in which they would like to participate.

Building the Theme

(30 minutes)

1. Call to Worship. For this activity provide Bibles, poster board, and a marker. Write the following Scripture references on the poster board: Hebrews 13:7; Hebrews 13:17; Titus 3:1; Romans 13:1; and Romans 13:5. Have the pupils look up these verses to see what they say about leadership. Have them take turns writing the verses in their own words on the poster board. **What do these verses tell us about authority?** (We are to obey and respect our leaders and submit to their authority.)

To begin the worship time, let pupils from Group 1 take turns reading what they have written.

Put Them in Order!

Read 1 Samuel 8, 9, 10. Then number these events in the proper order.

- ☐ Saul wanted to return home when the donkeys weren't found but the servant wanted to go see the prophet.
- ☐ Samuel anointed Saul with oil and received instructions.
- ☐ Samuel told the people the king would be harsh with the Israelites.
- ☐ Saul was chosen to be king but was hiding in the baggage.
- ☐ Saul ate with Samuel.
- ☐ Saul went home and kept silent.
- ☐ Saul and the servant met some girls and asked where the "seer" was.
- ☐ The Israelites asked Samuel for a king.
- ☐ Saul joined in prophesying at Gibeah.
- ☐ Samuel told Saul where the donkeys were and invited him to dinner.
- ☐ The people shouted, "Long live the king!"
- ☐ God told Samuel to give the Israelites a king.
- ☐ Samuel talked with Saul on the roof of his house.
- ☐ Samuel told the Israelites to present themselves before the Lord by tribes and clans.
- ☐ Saul's father asked Saul to take a servant and go look for the lost donkeys.
- ☐ Samuel explained the regulations of the kingship and wrote them on a scroll.
- ☐ The servant left and Saul stayed to receive a message from God.
- ☐ Samuel saw Saul and God told Samuel Saul was to be the king.

Activity Page 9A

2. Puppet Play. This activity could be a challenge activity. You will need small paper bags (lunch size), markers, construction paper, scissors, glue, paper, and pencils. The pupils will make paper-bag puppets and write short skits showing obedience to leadership. If your group is large, divide into two groups and do two skits. A group will work together on one skit—some doing the writing and others making the puppets. You may want to divide the group for the presentation—some working the puppets while others read the lines. During *Sharing in Worship*, the pupils will present their puppet play(s) immediately after the Call to Worship.

Focus a discussion on helping the pupils understand what represents leadership and why they should obey it. **Who are some leaders in your life at home? school? church? your community?** (Parents, teachers, principals, ministers, elders, deacons, police, and so on.) **Why do you need to obey these leaders?** (God tells us to; they know what is best; we need to obey our leaders so we can all get along.)

3. Devotion. For this activity you will need copies of Activity Page 9A, pencils, and Bibles. Have the pupils read the text from 1 Samuel. Then have them number the events found on their activity page in the correct order. As the children work, discuss the events to help them understand the order of the story. Let each pupil choose an event and illustrate it to show after the Devotion. Help the children choose key events from the story.

4. Scripture. For this activity provide copies of Activity Page 9B, pencils, and Bibles. Have the pupils look up the Scriptures to discover people in the Bible who were leaders. Have pupils write one or two sentences about these people. As the pupils work, discuss with them some of the characteristics of these leaders. Point out what made these people good leaders and discuss why God said they were to be respected. During *Sharing in Worship*, pupils will take turns sharing what they wrote about these Bible leaders.

5. Personal Praise. Have the pupils create some role plays about leaders. During *Sharing in Worship,* the pupils may present these role plays and have the other pupils guess who the leaders are. (For example: teacher, police, parent, and so on.)

Option: Let each pupil (or pair of pupils) choose an authority figure to pantomime. For example, a mother could shake her finger at the child and point as though telling the child to go to his or her room. A policeman could wave his arms as though directing traffic. A minister could hold up the Bible and preach. Or, a child might sit and read the Bible, showing God as the final authority.

Help the pupils think of various leaders in their lives. **Who are your leaders or authority figures at home?** (Parents.) **Who are your leaders at school?** (Teachers, principals, coaches.) **At church?** (Ministers, elders, deacons.) **In your community?** (Police, mayor, president.) **Who is our ultimate authority?** (God.)

6. Prayer. Copies of Activity Page 9C and pencils will be used in this activity. Have the pupils solve the puzzle on the activity page to find ways we can follow leaders. If you have time during the worship period for more group participation, make an enlarged copy of page 9C (either enlarge it on a photocopier or by hand). During *Sharing in Worship,* have pupils from Group 6 take turns filling in the blanks as the large group comes up with answers. This activity will end with prayer. See *Sharing in Worship* for prayer suggestions.

Help the children think of what all is involved in following leaders. **What are some ways we can follow our leaders?** (Obey them; show respect; and so on.) **How can we show respect to our leaders?** (Allow response. Speak kindly of them; use correct titles; do what they say; and so on.)

Sharing in Worship
(20-25 minutes)

Omit any of the following if you did not offer the corresponding activity. The Devotion can be used without the group activity.

Call to Worship (Group 1): **Group 1 has read some Scriptures about how we should relate to leaders. Group 1 will read their paraphrases of these verses.** Group 1 reads their sentences. **Today we want to worship God because He helps us follow our leaders.**

Puppet Play (Group 2): **Group 2 made puppets and wrote a short skit(s) about showing obedience to leadership.** Have the pupils present their puppet skits.

Devotion (Group 3): **Group 3 studied the story of King Saul's appointment to be king. After our Devotion they will show us some illustrations of our Bible story.**

The Israelites once again were disobedient to God. They were serving false gods and now they were wanting an earthly king to lead them. God told Samuel to warn them how harsh a king would be. He did so, but the people still wanted a king.

Saul was the man chosen by God to be the king. The day before Samuel met Saul, God told Samuel about him. "About this time tomorrow, I will send a young man to you who will deliver my people from the Philistines," God said. When Samuel saw Saul the next day, God said, "This is the man I told you about."

Saul sat down to a feast with Samuel; then Samuel anointed Saul king by pouring oil on his head. Later, Samuel gathered the people together and told them a king had been chosen. Samuel had the people present themselves by tribes and clans. When they couldn't find Saul, the Lord said the man was hiding among the baggage. The people

brought him out and shouted, "Long live the king!" Samuel explained the regulations of kingship and wrote them on a scroll. Everyone went home, including Saul. Some were happy with this man while others hated him.

How do you think Saul felt? (Allow response.) **What a big responsibility to be king over all those people! Do you still think God chooses who will be our leaders?** (Allow response.) **God is always in control. He knows who our leaders are going to be. And God has given us a definite command on how we are to treat our leaders. We have already heard some things about how we are supposed to treat our leaders.** (Let pupils tell what they remember.) **It is very simple: we are to respect them and submit to them. God knew our world would be a disaster without leadership. God also knows that, in order for leaders to be effective, we must respect and obey them. God always knows what is best for us.**

Group 3 should show their illustrations of the story now.

Scripture (Group 4): **Group 4 researched some other Bible leaders.** Have the children take turns sharing what they wrote about the Bible leaders.

Lord's Supper: God has told us to obey our leaders and submit to their authority. We should obey God because He always knows what is best for us. God has also told us to take the Lord's Supper and remember Jesus and what He did for us. As we take the Lord's Supper, let's remember how Jesus suffered and died for us.

Offering: As we give our offerings today, let's pray for our church leaders. Let's ask God to give our leaders the wisdom to use the money in a way that will please God.

Personal Praise (Group 5): **Group 5 has some role plays to share with us about leaders.** Have the pupils present the role plays. The others may try to guess who the leader is. (Example: teacher, parent, minister, and so on.)

Prayer (Group 6): **Group 6 solved a puzzle to find ways we can follow our leaders.** Have the pupils take turns telling ways to obey leadership. After pupils have finished, have a time of guided prayer. First, suggest that pupils thank God for your church leaders. Then suggest that they pray for your church leaders to be effective leaders. Then have pupils pray that they might respect and obey your church leaders. To close, have an adult offer an audible prayer praising God for helping everyone follow leaders.

Closing Moments
• • • • • • • • • • • • • • • • • • • •
(10-15 minutes)

Write a Letter. You will need to provide stationery, stamps, and pens or pencils. Have each pupil think of a leader who is important to him or her. When pupils have made their choices, help them write letters thanking these people for being leaders. If anyone chooses a person such as the President, you will need to find the proper address and mail the letter yourself.

Put Them in Order!

Read 1 Samuel 8, 9, 10. Then number these events in the proper order.

☐ Saul wanted to return home when the donkeys weren't found but the servant wanted to go see the prophet.

☐ Samuel anointed Saul with oil and received instructions.

☐ Samuel told the people the king would be harsh with the Israelites.

☐ Saul was chosen to be king but was hiding in the baggage.

☐ Saul ate with Samuel.

☐ Saul went home and kept silent.

☐ Saul and the servant met some girls and asked where the "seer" was.

☐ The Israelites asked Samuel for a king.

☐ Saul joined in prophesying at Gibeah.

☐ Samuel told Saul where the donkeys were and invited him to dinner.

☐ The people shouted, "Long live the king!"

☐ God told Samuel to give the Israelites a king.

☐ Samuel talked with Saul on the roof of his house.

☐ Samuel told the Israelites to present themselves before the Lord by tribes and clans.

☐ Saul's father asked Saul to take a servant and go look for the lost donkeys.

☐ Samuel explained the regulations of the kingship and wrote them on a scroll.

☐ The servant left and Saul stayed to receive a message from God.

☐ Samuel saw Saul and God told Samuel Saul was to be the king.

Look in the Bible to find out something about these leaders. Draw a line from each reference to the leader, and a line from the leader to the phrase describing him or her.

Exodus 4:10	Aaron	risked life for people
Exodus 32:2-4	Esther	had trouble speaking
Esther 3:5, 6	Saul	made an idol
Esther 4:15, 16	Moses	claimed the power of God against the enemy
1 Samuel 15:24, 25	Haman	asked God for discerning heart
1 Samuel 17:45	Solomon	wanted to destroy the Jews
1 Kings 3:6-9	David	gave in to the people

Follow the Leader

Choose to Follow

Solve the puzzle to find ways we can follow our leaders. The consonants are given. Place the vowels at the end of each line in the correct blanks.

1. __ b __ y l __ ws (aeo)
2. __ nc __ __ r __ g __   __ d __ lts t __ v __ t __ (aaeeeooouu)
3. p __ y t __ x __ s (aae)
4. b __ y l __ c __ ns __ s (eeiu)
5. pr __ y f __ r l __ __ d __ rs (aaeeo)
6. r __ sp __ ct l __ __ d __ rs (aeeee)
7. d __ n't s __ y b __ d th __ ngs __ b __ __ t l __ __ d __ rs (aaaaeeioou)
8. __ s __ t __ tl __ s __ f r __ sp __ ct (eeeeiou)
9. l __ st __ n t __ l __ __ d __ rs (aeeeio)
10. __ nc __ __ r __ g __ l __ __ d __ rs (aaeeeeou)

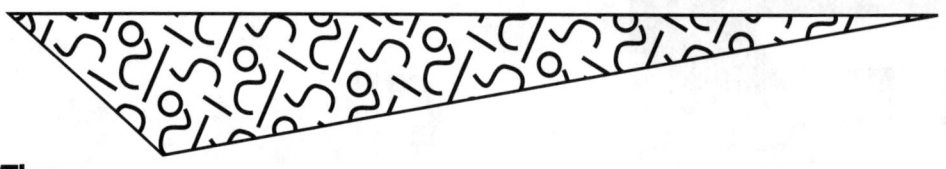

Unit Three
Leaders Please God
Scripture Text: 1 Samuel 16:3-7, 10-13

Session 10

An Obedient Heart

Worship Focus

Worship God because He knows and cares about what is in our hearts.

Transition Time
(10-15 minutes)

Allow pupils time to use the rest rooms and drinking fountain.

I Didn't Know That! When pupils return, serve heart-shaped candies or cookies. Or serve another kind of snack from a heart-shaped dish. Give out pencils and slips of paper to pupils. **Write a fun fact about yourself that no one in this group will know.** (For example: I like liver; I can roll my tongue; I can speak Spanish.) Put the slips of paper in a bag or box. Have one pupil at a time draw out a slip and read it. The other pupils should guess whose slip of paper it is.

We often think we know almost everything about our friends; but we really don't. Even if we lived with them, or had a hidden camera observing them, we still wouldn't know them as well as God knows each of us.

Launching the Theme
(10 minutes)

This month we will be looking at people's hearts and motivations for doing things. I'm not talking about Valentines' Day hearts. I'm talking about your spiritual heart, the part that makes decisions to choose good or evil—the center of your thoughts and feelings. Ask for volunteers to read Proverbs 4:23 and 27:19.

For the next four weeks, we'll be looking at the hearts of some of God's leaders. We'll also discover what to do to make our hearts pleasing to God. Today's focus is on the prophet Samuel. Samuel had an obedient heart. He always tried to please God. When he was just a boy the Bible says, "The Lord was with Samuel as he grew up, and he let none of his words fall to the ground" (1 Samuel 3:19). **How can we have obedient hearts? We'll find out today, as we worship God because He knows and cares what is in our hearts.**

Take time to explain the choices for the *Building the Theme* activities. Allow pupils to choose the groups in which they would like to participate.

Building the Theme

(30 minutes)

1. Call to Worship. Pupils will write a personal paraphrase of Psalm 139:1-6. Provide paper, pencils, Bibles, markers or crayons, or overhead transparencies and pens, and copies of Activity Page 10A. Make copies for the entire group. The other pupils can fill theirs out at home. Ask several members of Group 1 to pass out the pages to the large group after the Call to Worship.

Talk with the pupils about their daily activities. Draw a large clock on the chalkboard (set to 8 a.m.). **Let's take a moment to think about the activities in your day. What do you usually do each hour?** As pupils talk about what they do, fill in the various hours.

Have a pupil read aloud Psalm 139:6. **How do these verses make you feel? Are you happy that God knows and cares about you so much? Does it make you feel nervous?**

We will use page 10A to write our own paraphrases for these verses. Using the words and ideas from the discussion, each pupil will have a personal paraphrase of Psalm 139:1-6. Ask a few pupils to read their paraphrases as the Call to Worship.

2. Music. Pupils will sing the songs, "Into My Heart" and "Lord, I Want to Be a Christian." They will also write new stanzas to the latter. If these songs are unfamiliar to you or to your pupils, choose others that mention the heart.

Provide Bibles, tape player, and tape. Before class, tape record the music to both songs. If you or someone else you know is familiar with sign language, make plans to teach the pupils how to sign the original chorus of "Lord, I Want to Be a Christian."

What does this song say about our commitment to God? It begins in our hearts. That's where real change takes place. When we are committed to God, it's a total commitment. What are some other words we could sing about our hearts' commitment? (For example: "Lord, I want to be like Jesus [more loving; more caring; love like You do; care like You do] in my heart." Or, "Lord, I want You first of all in my heart.")

3. Scripture. Pupils will solve simple math problems to decipher 1 Samuel 16:7, and identify ways God looks at their hearts. Provide Bibles, pencils, and copies of Activity Page 10B.

There are many things we can know about each other. We don't even have to talk—we can tell just by looking. But God knows much more about us. Let's read about this in 1 Samuel 16:7. Before you open your Bibles, however, work the problems at the top of the activity page to see what the verse says.

Once pupils have completed the top portion of Activity Page 10B, have them follow the instructions to complete the bottom of the page. Help pupils decide how they will present their material during *Sharing in Worship*.

4. Lord's Supper. Pupils will help in a scientific demonstration to use during *Sharing in Worship*. For each pupil, provide a pair of scissors, a plastic or paper cup half filled with water, a disk-type coffee filter, and a water-soluble black marker.

We've talked about how God sees each heart. He doesn't just see part of it—He sees every thought, word, action, deed. That's incredible when you think about how involved each person's life is!

Look at your markers. What color are they? Yes, they look black. But we're going to show that things aren't always what they appear to be.

Have pupils cut their filters into heart shapes and mark all around the hearts with the black markers. Then have them put the tips of the hearts in the cups of water. (Try this experiment at home ahead of time. The black marks should separate into different colors. Capillary action forces the water up the filter and dissolves the components of the ink.)

Leave the hearts at the edge of the cups so the tips of the filters are in the water. After this, ask a pupil to read 1 Samuel 16:6, 7. The pupils will present their findings during the Lord's Supper talk.

5. Devotion. The pupils will read Scriptures that show God is more concerned about inner purity (of the heart) than outward actions. You'll need a large sheet of paper or poster board, scissors, Bibles, and pencils or markers. Also, have a large sheet of paper or poster board and Plasti-Tak® or tape for the pupils to use to put the heart puzzle together during *Sharing in Worship*. If you have a bulletin board handy, use that.

Ahead of time, draw a large heart on paper or poster board. Have a list of appropriate Scriptures ready. (A list of possible Scriptures is given below. Use a concordance to help you find more "heart" Scriptures.) In class, divide the heart into as many pieces as you have pupils in this group. On each piece, write a Scripture reference. Cut the heart into pieces. (Possible Scriptures include: Proverbs 2:2; 3:5; 4:23; 15:13; 16:23; 23:17; 23:19; 27:19; Psalms 51:10; 66:18; 86:11; 119:11; 119:12; 139:23.)

Give each pupil a puzzle piece. **This Scripture will tell you what God's priority is concerning our hearts. How does this verse help us understand what kind of heart God wants us to have? After you think for a moment, use the crayons or markers to illustrate the verse on a sheet of paper.**

During *Sharing in Worship*, pupils can put up their heart puzzle pieces, read their Scriptures aloud, and show their illustrations. Plan to display these for the next four weeks.

6. Heartfelt Prayers. Pupils will write sentence prayers to use in a group prayer session during *Sharing in Worship*. Provide Bibles, paper, and pencils.

Sometimes we think that people won't like us if we're really honest and tell what's in our hearts. God knows everything about us and He still loves us.

Ask a pupil to read Jeremiah 17:10. Then ask the pupils to finish this statement on their papers: "Lord, help my heart to be more _____ like Yours is."

During the Prayer portion of *Sharing in Worship*, a pupil will read Jeremiah 17:10. Then other volunteers may read their prayer statements as part of a group prayer. Have an adult close the prayer session.

Sharing in Worship
(20-25 minutes)

Call to Worship (Group 1): **Group 1 has prepared personal paraphrases of Psalm 139:1-6. As our call to worship today, some volunteers will read theirs now.** Have three or four volunteers read their paraphrases. After they have finished, have designated pupils pass out copies of page 10A to the entire group.

Special Music (Group 2): **Group 2 will lead us in some songs about our hearts.** Have Group 2 lead the song, "Into My Heart." Then have the group lead the song, "Lord, I Want to Be a Christian" and teach the new stanzas of the song.

Scripture (Group 3): **Group 3 has worked some math problems to discover a very important Scripture verse and what it means to us. They will present their material now.**

Lord's Supper (Group 4): **Group 4 will show the results from a scientific experiment that they started.** Have pupils show their coffee filters. (By now, the black marks will have separated into different colors.) **Although the marks we put on the filters were black to start with, they have changed to show us that black is a combination of all other colors.**

Let's take time to think about the condition of our own hearts. Our friends may see only one side of our hearts. (Show a black marker; then hold up a wet filter.) **But God sees through the black to all the colors—all the things in our hearts that cause us to behave the way we do. God sent His Son, Jesus, to die for our sins. He has made our hearts pure and acceptable to God. Right now, talk to God privately about the condition of your heart and thank Him for sending Jesus to be your Savior.**

Offering: Ask pupils to collect the offering at this time.

Devotion (Group 5): **Group 5 will present Scriptures that show God is more concerned about inner purity of the heart than any outward actions.** Group 5 members should read their Scripture verses, put up their heart puzzle pieces, and then show their illustrations

The Bible contains at least six hundred references to the word *heart*. **By this we know that God thought the heart was very important. Throughout the Bible and other literature, the heart was considered the main source for a person's emotions and feelings. In reality, you have a physical heart—a large muscle that pumps blood into the rest of your body to keep you alive. But you also have a spiritual heart that helps to keep you spiritually healthy so you can make the right choices.**

The same good things that keep your physical heart healthy also keep your spiritual heart healthy! (Make large signs of the following topics and display them to illustrate your points.)

1. *Good Food*—**Just as your physical heart needs nourishment, so does your spiritual heart. Your spiritual heart gets strong when you "feed" it by thinking about and learning from God's Word.**

2. *Exercise*—**Just as your physical heart needs exercise to remain strong, your spiritual heart does too. Caring for others, being kind, showing love to others—these are ways to exercise your spiritual heart.**

3. *Less Junk Food*—**You know for a fact that a steady diet of junk food is bad for your physical heart, and it can raise your cholesterol level! It's the same with your spiritual heart—a steady diet of junk food, such as questionable movies or magazines, or activities such as jealousy or gossip, can clog your spiritual arteries and weaken your spiritual heart.**

The Bible calls Jesus the Great Physician. He's the One to go to for help with a heart problem.

Prayer (Group 6): **Group 6 will be leading our heartfelt prayers now.** Group 6 can begin the sentence prayers. Encourage each to pray this prayer: "Lord, help my heart to be more _____." Then close the prayer time.

Closing Moments
• • • • • • • • • • • • • • • • • • •
(10-15 minutes)

Heart Reminders. Pupils will make prayer and devotion reminders for the week. Provide Bibles, pencils, scissors, and envelopes. Also have copies of Activity Page 10C so pupils can write a Scripture reference on each heart puzzle piece, cut out the heart pieces, and put them in the envelopes.

Challenge pupils to take out one piece each day, read the Scripture, and write down a word or two about the reference on the puzzle piece. Next week, you may want to provide some sort of incentive (stickers or heart-shape candy) for pupils who bring their puzzles back with all the Scriptures read.

One of a Kind

Read Psalm 139:1-6. Fill in the blanks to write your own personal psalm to God.

Oh Lord, You have searched me and know me. You know when I
_____
_____
and when I _____
_____
You know when I go _____
_____
and when I _____
Before I _____,
You know _____.
You protect me from _____,
and _____.
This news is so wonderful, I _____.
_____
But it makes me want to _____.

Thank You, God.

Love,

_____

10A © 1994 by The STANDARD PUBLISHING COMPANY. Permission is granted to photocopy this page for ministry purposes only—not for resale.

GOD'S VIEW of You

God sees you in a special way that no one else can. Solve the math problems to choose the correct words to fill in the blanks. Then check your Bible to see if you're right.

1. the
2. at
3. not
4. Lord
5. man
6. outward
7. things
8. appearance
9. but
10. heart
11. does
12. look

3 - 2 = ◯   2 + 2 = ◯   10 + 1 = ◯   2 + 1 = ◯   6 + 6 = ◯

1 + 1 = ◯   5 - 4 = ◯   3 + 4 = ◯   7 - 2 = ◯   8 + 4 = ◯ s

3 - 1 = ◯ .   4 + 1 = ◯   10 + 2 = ◯ s   2 + 0 = ◯   8 - 7 = ◯

3 + 3 = ◯   9 - 1 = ◯   3 + 6 = ◯ ,   6 - 5 = ◯   5 - 1 = ◯

12 + 0 = ◯ s   6 - 4 = ◯   12 - 11 = ◯   5 + 5 = ◯ .

-- 1 Samuel 16:7

There are things people can tell about you just by looking, even if you don't say anything. But God knows much more about you. Next to each item below, draw a ⇧ if it's something God knows about you. Draw a ☺ if it's something other people can see.

- color of my eyes
- how I feel
- my deepest secret
- length of my hair
- if I'm thankful
- shape of my nose

- what I'm thinking right now
- size of my feet
- reasons why I do what I do
- my gender—girl or boy
- when I need forgiveness
- clothes I'm wearing

Heart Surgery

Write one of the following Scripture references on each puzzle piece. Then cut apart the heart. Each day of the coming week, take one of the pieces, read the Scripture, and write one or two words to help you remember what it says. This will help you strengthen your heart.

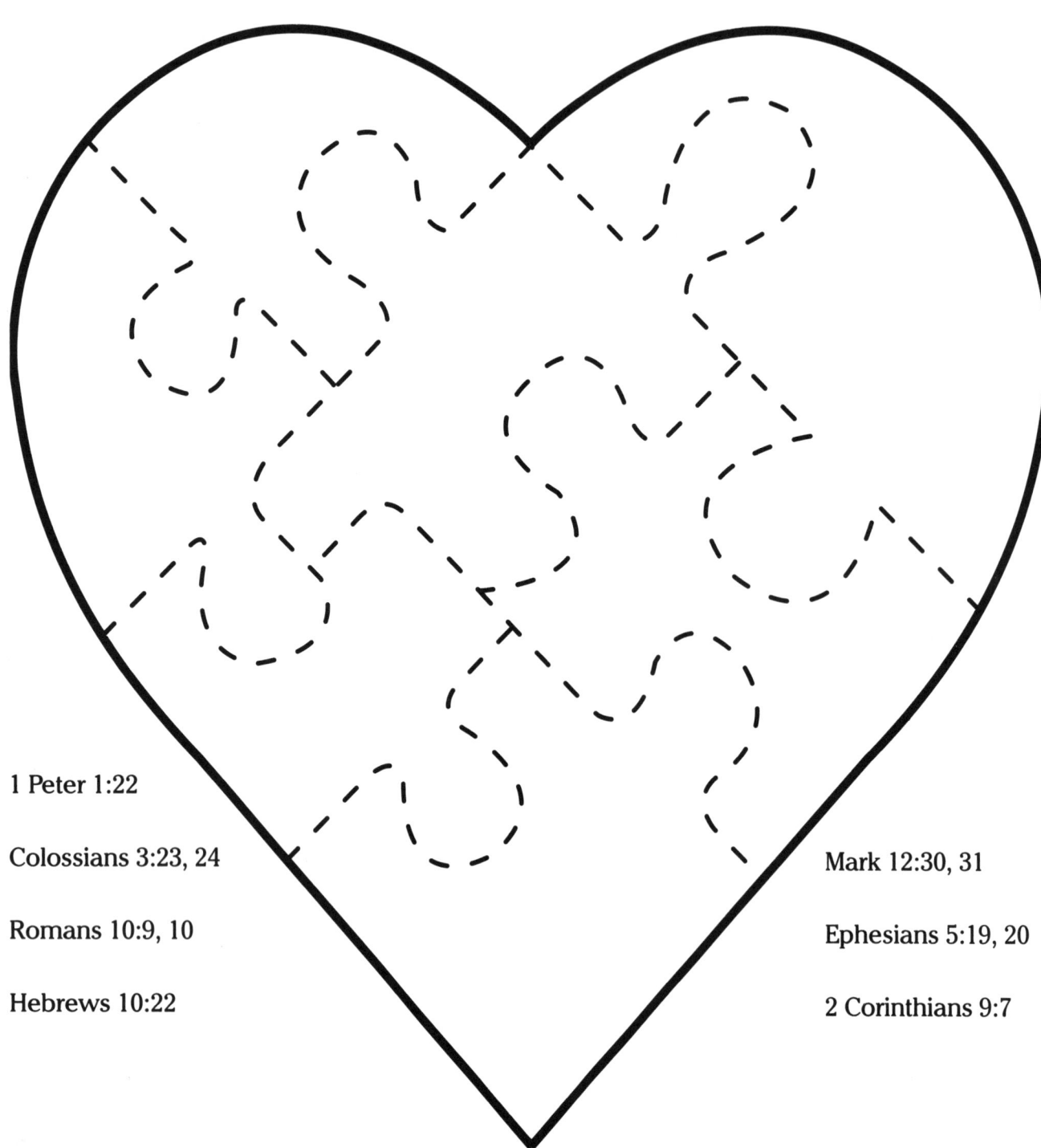

1 Peter 1:22

Colossians 3:23, 24

Romans 10:9, 10

Hebrews 10:22

Mark 12:30, 31

Ephesians 5:19, 20

2 Corinthians 9:7

Unit Three
Leaders Please God
Scripture Text: 1 Samuel 19:1, 2; 20:1, 4, 17, 18, 24, 27, 30-33, 35, 42; 2 Samuel 8:15; 9:1, 3, 5-7

Session 11

A Loving Heart

Worship Focus

Worship God because He is a friend who knows our hearts and accepts us as we are.

Transition Time
(10-15 minutes)

Friendship Graffiti. Have a large sheet of newsprint hung on the wall. Across the top write, "A friend is someone who . . . " Provide several markers and ask each pupil to finish the statement about what makes a good friend. If there is time, allow pupils to add decorations to your "Friendship Graffiti."

Launching the Theme
(10 minutes)

Provide a variety of greeting cards that friends might send to each other, or copy the messages from greeting cards onto poster board. Distribute the cards to the pupils. Call attention to the "Friendship Graffiti" that pupils just completed. Read several of the statements aloud or comment upon the many good ideas the pupils came up with about friendship. **Friends also like to send and receive greeting cards. Let's think about the kinds of cards friends send and the occasions that friends send each other cards.**

Ask each pupil to describe an occasion when his or her card or a message from the board might be sent to a friend. Also ask pupils to think of times people show friendship to each other (birthdays, special holidays, sickness, when they need help, when they did something special, to thank them).

Today we are celebrating the friendship between David and Jonathan and the friendship David had with God; and our friendship with others and our friendship with God. We will worship God because He is a friend who knows our hearts and accepts us as we are.

Building the Theme
(30 minutes)

1. Call to Worship. Pupils will write a paraphrase of 1 Corinthians 13:4-7, using words that relate to things that friends do. Provide paper, pencils, several translations of the Bible, and copies of Activity Page 11A.

First Corinthians 13 is sometimes called the "Love Chapter." It tells ways a loving Christian responds to others. Look at verses 4 through 7 to see how these loving responses can help us in our relationships with friends.

Take time to read 1 Corinthians 13:4-7 from several translations so you can compare them. Then, using page 11A, rewrite the verses to show loving ways friends can respond to each other.

Have the pupils practice reading their paraphrases aloud, or work as a group on one paraphrase and read it together as a group for the Call to Worship during *Sharing in Worship.*

2. Special Music. Pupils will sing the song, "What a Friend We Have in Jesus," during the Lord's Supper meditation. They will also write a song about friendship using the melody of the song, "They Will Know We Are Christians." They should be prepared to teach the new song if time allows.

Provide Bibles, hymn and chorus books, pencils, and paper. It would also be helpful to have a tape player and cassette tape with these two songs so pupils can practice singing with the tape. If desired, write out the new words on an overhead transparency or on the chalkboard for the whole group to see.

Go over the words to "What a Friend We Have in Jesus" to make sure the group knows them. Then listen to the song, "They Will Know We Are Christians." Brainstorm about things that friends do for others. (Suggestions might include: "They will know we are friends by our love [care, joy, hope, etc.]")

Practice singing the song with the new words. Then, if there is time, ask pupils to use paper and crayons to illustrate the key words to the song—love, care, etc.

During *Sharing in Worship,* pupils from Group 3 will share their new stanzas, show their illustrations, and sing the song with the entire group.

3. Scripture. Pupils will investigate several Scriptures about the condition of David's heart that also may apply to their own hearts. Provide Bibles, pencils, and copies of Activity Page 11B.

Our friends cannot see inside our hearts—they only see the results or actions from what's going on inside. But God sees inside our hearts to understand what we're really like, and what our motivations are. On our activity page are some hearts with problems. You be the doctor and prescribe what these hearts need by looking at the Scripture references.

Ask volunteers to look up and read aloud the Scripture references; then discuss the condition of each heart, and decide on the "prescription" or cure for it. Have the group compile a list of suggestions from these Scriptures that would help to strengthen their own hearts.

4. Offering. This group will prepare mobiles to display during the Offering. For each pupil, you'll need one coat hanger or dowel rod, string or yarn, markers or crayons, pencils, scissors, a copy of Activity Page 11C printed on heavy paper or cardboard.

Pupils should cut out the letters. Then brainstorm to come up with words or phrases that describe friends, and that begin with these letters. Some examples of words or phrases might include:

F—Friendly, fun, fun to be with;
R—Responsible, respectful, respects my opinions;
I—Interesting, inspiring, interesting to be with;
E—Encouraging, excellent, eager to share with me;
N—Nice, neighbor, nice to be with;
D—Dear, disciple of Jesus, does nice things for me.

Ask pupils to write a word or phrase on each letter and decorate the letter with markers or crayons. Use tape to suspend the letters on the hanger or dowel rod with the yarn or string.

During the Offering, pupils will display their mobiles, read the words and phrases, and tell why these are important qualities for friends. Make sure the pupils in this group understand what they will be doing, so they will be prepared to speak about their projects.

5. Devotion. Pupils will create and present "snapshot scenes" to illustrate examples of Bible friendships. Provide Bibles, and Bible costumes for skits. Or provide Bibles, poster board and markers or crayons, so pupil pairs can illustrate the scenes from the Bible.

Have the pairs work together to read the Scripture references and then come up with two or three minutes of dialogue. Use the following references and Scripture friends:

David and Jonathan (friends are unselfish)—1 Samuel 18:1-4; 19:1-7; 20:32-42.
Ruth and Naomi (friends can be any age or race)—Ruth 1:15-22.
Ananias and Saul (enemies can become friends)—Acts 9:10-19.
Jesus and Peter (friends forgive)—Luke 22:54-62; Mark 16:6, 7.
Jesus, Mary, and Martha (friends are truthful)—Luke 10:38-42.

These groups will present their dialogues during the Devotion. Ask the large group to guess the identity of these friends by listening to the dialogues.

6. Friendly Prayers. This first idea will involve more-mature pupils. A simpler idea is suggested under "Option."

Before class, assemble a variety of objects in a paper bag. They should be things that could be used to remind someone of friends. For example, a balloon, a whistle, a pencil, a Bible, food or a picture of food, and so forth. A pupil will draw an object from the bag, and then describe how a friend is like that object, using this format: "A friend is like (or reminds me of) a whistle because it gets attention when you blow it. Thank You, God, for giving us friends who pay attention to us."

Option: For a simpler activity, have pupils write prayers about friends using the following Scriptures: Proverbs 18:24b; 17:17a; 27:10; John 15:14, 15. For example: "There is a friend who sticks closer than a brother. Thank You, God, for being that kind of a friend."

Pupils will express their prayer thoughts at the end of *Sharing in Worship.*

Sharing Worship
(20-25 minutes)

Call to Worship (Group 1): **Group 1 has prepared their own paraphrase of 1 Corinthians 13:4-7 to show how friends lovingly respond to others. Group 1 will read their paraphrase(s) now.**

Special Music (Group 2): **Group 2 has prepared a special number for us.** Group 2 sings "They Will Know We Are Friends" and shares their illustrations for the new words to the song. Then ask the whole group to sing the song with them.

Scripture (Group 3): **Group 3 investigated verses from Psalms that talk about heart conditions.** Let each member have a turn to be the "doctor" and share a diagnosis and a prescription.

Lord's Supper: Let's take this time to think about our best friend, Jesus. Would you die for any of your friends? Would any of them give their lives for you? Jesus did that for us. He gave His life to take away the sin in our lives. Listen as Group 3 sings "What a Friend We Have in Jesus." Then talk to Him and thank Him for being the best friend you will ever have.

Offering (Group 4): Pray that the offering may be used to help friends know about Jesus. While the offering is being passed, ask volunteers from this group to show their mobiles and share their words and phrases about friends.

Devotion (Group 5): **At the beginning of the session we talked about ways that**

we could show friendship and about what friendship involves. **Group 5 has prepared some scenes that show how Bible characters showed friendship to each other. Try to guess who these people are.** Let each group present their skit; then stress the following points.

Each of these groups presented a different aspect of friendship. Let's examine each one for a few minutes. Have each aspect written on a piece of poster board or on the chalkboard and unveil it at the proper time. Have pupils from Group 5 prepared to read the Scriptures at the appropriate times.

1. Friends are unselfish. **Jonathan risked his own life to save David's life. You may never be called upon to risk your life for a friend, but there will be times when you will be inconvenienced by your friends. But that is part of what friendship is about. Look at how unselfish Jesus was—He died for His friends. That includes you and me!** A pupil reads John 15:14, 15.

2. Friends can be any age and any race. **Ruth and Naomi were friends even though they were from different countries, were different generations, and had different needs. Do all your friends look just like you? Do you have friends of different races, ages, sizes? Remember, God does not judge us by our outward appearances but by our hearts.** A pupil reads 1 Samuel 16:7.

3. Enemies can become friends. **Ananias knew that Saul had been killing Christians. But he was commanded by God to help him, and through God's power Ananias helped Saul. Do you have enemies? How do you treat them? How do you feel about them in your heart? Remember that we were enemies to God when Jesus died for us.** A pupil reads Romans 5:8.

4. Friends forgive. **Although Peter and Jesus were close friends, Peter turned his back on Jesus when He needed a friend. But Jesus forgave Peter, and He continues to forgive us.** A pupil reads 1 John 1:8. **Do you need to ask for or grant some forgiveness today?**

5. Friends are truthful. **Martha really wanted everything to be just right for Jesus, and she was very upset with Mary for not helping. But Jesus had to be honest and tell Martha she needed to rearrange her priorities. Have you ever had to be really honest with a friend? Did telling the truth strengthen your friendship? Jesus, our best friend, always tells us the truth.** A pupil reads Hebrews 13:8.

Prayer (Group 6): **Group 6 will be thanking God for giving us friends and for being our best friend.** Have volunteers read their prayer ideas. Then close the prayer time yourself.

Closing Moments
(10-15 minutes)

Prayer Partners. The object of this activity is to show that two people can be friends and pray for each other even though they have differences as well as similarities. Make a list of the boys and girls in your class. Put the boys' names in one bag and the girls' names in another. Give each pupil a piece of paper and a pencil. Draw out names so that all pupils are paired off, boys with boys and girls with girls.

The pairs should work together to find out three things they have in common and three things that are different.

Ask the pairs to say sentence prayers for each other before they leave, and/or at home during the week.

Friendtalk

Read 1 Corinthians 13:4-7. Then finish the sentences below in your own words.

Love is patient and kind. I want to be a loving friend, so I will _____
_____
my friends. A loving friend is not _____ or self-seeking, and does not get angry easily, so I will try _____
_____

Since loving friends are not happy with evil, but _____
_____, I will be happy when _____
_____

Love patiently accepts all things. When my friend _____
_____, I will _____

Since love trusts and hopes I will keep working on my friendship to _____
_____, even when it's hard.

To the Rescue!

Check the vital signs on these heart conditions, then come up with a prescription from God's Word.

Divided heart
℞: Psalm 86:11, 12
_____
_____
_____
_____

Weak heart
℞: Psalm 28:7
_____
_____
_____
_____

Faint heart
℞: Psalm 61:2, 3
_____
_____
_____
_____

Broken heart
℞: Psalm 34:17, 18
_____
_____
_____
_____

Fearful heart
℞: Psalm 112:6-8
_____
_____
_____
_____

Unhappy heart
℞: Psalm 19:7, 8
_____
_____
_____
_____

Longing heart
℞: Psalm 37:3, 4
_____
_____
_____
_____

Foolish heart
℞: Psalm 90:12
_____
_____
_____
_____

Write on these letters words that describe friends. Decorate the letters with markers or crayons, and make a mobile using a dowel rod or wire clothes hanger.

Unit Three
Leaders Please God
Scripture Text: 1 Kings 3:5-15

Session 12

A Wise Heart

Worship Focus

Worship God because He gives wisdom and direction.

Transition Time
(10-15 minutes)

Treasure Hunt. Ahead of time, hide some money in the room. Tell the pupils they can keep any money they find. After the money is found, ask a pupil to read Proverbs 2:1-5.

I could tell by watching you that everyone really wanted to find the money! Do you look for spiritual treasures as enthusiastically as you did today's material treasure? Spiritual treasures are plentiful in the Bible, where we find wisdom and direction for our lives. That passage in Proverbs told us to search for understanding and wisdom just like we would hunt for silver and treasure.

Launching the Theme
(10 minutes)

Divide the class into teams. Provide paper and pencils. Give pupils two minutes to list as many kinds of light as they can think of. (For example: search, flash, spot, fire, ultra violet, night, day, lantern, fluorescent, northern, infra red.)

Why is light essential to our lives? (Without light, there would be no life. Our planet would be a frozen ice ball without the sun. Plants and flowers can't live without light. In winter, when there are fewer daylight hours, some people get depressed and are treated with light therapy. Light is essential for life.) **The Bible says, "God is light and in him is no darkness at all" (1 John 1:5).**

Light is also essential to give us direction. When we are in the dark, we need to see where to go. You know how important it is to have flashlights or candles when the electricity goes off.

How do we get God's light in our lives? Not by sunbathing for several hours each day! We receive God's light and direction by reading and studying God's Word, the Bible. Psalm 119:105 says, "Your word is a lamp to my feet and a light to my path." Using God's Word is like shining a powerful light to see where you are going. It gives you direction. Today we will worship God because He gives wisdom and direction.

Building the Theme
(30 minutes)

1. Call to Worship. Pupils will work a crossword puzzle about wisdom from Proverbs 2. Provide Bibles, pencils, and copies of Activity Page 12A.

If I could grant you one wish, what would you ask for? If I went around the room, I'm sure I'd get lots of different answers. But I don't think anyone would ask for wisdom on the first try!

Wisdom has several definitions—the quality of being wise, having good judgment, having learning or knowledge. But it's not just a matter of being smart. Wise people realize they need God in their lives. They include God in their decisions—in all the important aspects of their lives.

After pupils work the puzzle and check their answers, ask them to practice reading Proverbs 2:1-5 aloud as a group. You may want to assign pupils to read the individual verses or read them all together. Pupils will read Proverbs 2:1-5 as the Call the Worship.

2. Special Music. This group will sing the song, "Thy Word Have I Hid in My Heart." Provide Bibles, hymn books or chorus books, pencils, paper, cassette tape and tape player. Ask a pupil to write the words on an overhead transparency (or chalkboard) so that all pupils can see the words. This will be the special music, just after the Call to Worship.

If possible, tape record the song ahead of time so pupils can practice with the tape. Ask a pupil to read Psalm 119:97-105. Then discuss with pupils. **How does the psalmist feel about God's Word? How did it help him?** (The psalmist loved God's Word. It made him wise, and gave him insight and understanding.) **God's Word can help us in many ways. It can help us make decisions and give us direction for our lives.**

NOTE: If your group has a more appropriate song or chorus about God's Word, use it. If it is very familiar you may want to ask pupils to write new stanzas for the song. Or use the young children's song, "The B-I-B-L-E," and ask this group to write new stanzas that they could teach the others. For example: "The B-I-B-L-E, yes that's the book for me, (It tells me how to live my life; It tells me how to love God more; It helps me do what I should do), the B-I-B-L-E."

3. Scripture. This group will investigate Scripture verses that tell the condition of Solomon's heart when he became king.

Ahead of time, prepare a large paper or poster-board heart cut into six pieces. Write one of these Scriptures on each piece:
1. 2 Chronicles 1:6 (he worshiped God).
2. 1 Kings 3:10 (he pleased God).
3. 1 Kings 10:7, 8 (his people were happy with him).
4. 1 Kings 3:7 (he was humble).
5. 1 Kings 3:9 (he asked for a discerning heart).
6. 1 Kings 6:1 (he built a temple for God).

Give a piece of the heart to each pupil or pair of pupils. Pupils will look up the verses to discover facts about Solomon; then write these facts on the pieces of the heart. They will report on their findings during the Scripture portion of *Sharing in Worship*.

4. Wisdom Watch. This activity will take some advance preparation. You may want to do this with a small group, or with the group as a whole during the Offering portion of *Sharing in Worship*.

Set up an obstacle course in your room with chairs, tables, etc. Darken the room as much as possible. Pupils will use flashlights to go through the course, stop at eight points, and follow written instructions that include reading Scriptures. Try to have an adult or teen at each stop to help the pupils. Here are the instructions to use along the way:

1. Have someone try to walk with a flashlight on his feet. Then read Psalm 119:105. Who is our real light? How does He do that?

2. Have someone try to move around with a Bible inside his shirt. Then read Psalm 119:11. How do you hide God's Word in your heart?

3. Have each person tell one thing of which he or she is really proud. Then read 1 Corinthians 1:30, 31. How can we boast in the Lord?

4. Name three or four sources to help us in our decision-making. Then read Psalm 51:6. To whom should we always go first?

5. Find a place where you can hide your whole class. It's not easy, is it? Then read Matthew 5:14. Why should we not try to hide from God?

6. Have an adult or teen light a small candle; then try to walk around while everyone blows on the candle. Then read Psalm 18:28. Who keeps our light shining?

7. Use a piece of play dough to make a model of the sun and moon (or, draw a picture). Is there any way we can make them shine? Who made the real sun and moon? Why? Read Psalm 74:16.

8. Each person must tell one thing that makes him or her happy. Read Psalm 97:11. Who is our real source of happiness? How can we remember that?

As pupils go through the "Wisdom Walk," ask them to think about why God is called Light. At the end, ask God for help in seeking His direction and guidance in our lives.

5. Devotion. This group will prepare a visual demonstration based on the parable from Matthew 7:24-27. Provide Bibles, paper, pencils, scissors, and construction paper. **Option:** If you prefer to act out the parable of the wise and foolish builders, use cardboard blocks.

Have pupils make tools and building materials from construction paper. Cut out two sets of materials so you can make two houses. Pupils should label the foundation, walls, roof, doors, and windows with names of things the wise person included in his life—Bible reading, praying, kindness, giving, going to church, witnessing; the foolish person—wrong friends, reading bad magazines and books, selfishness, jealousy, anger, not going to church, and so forth.

During the Devotion, pupils will help you illustrate your devotional talk.

6. Prayer. Pupils will write personal prayers using proverbs about wisdom. Provide Bibles, pencils, and copies of Activity Page 12B.

Let's see how good a wisdom seeker you are. See if you can match up these phrases about wisdom from the book of Proverbs—written by Solomon—*without* using your Bibles. Then use your Bibles to check your answers.

Do this activity individually or as a group. Then encourage each pupil to choose a favorite verse, put his or her name on the verse, and write a prayer based on it. During the prayer portion of *Sharing in Worship,* volunteers can read their prayers aloud.

Sharing in Worship
(20-25 minutes)

Call to Worship (Group 1): **Group 1 worked a crossword puzzle from Proverbs 2:1-5. As we begin our worship, Group 1 will read Proverbs 2:1-5. Listen carefully to find directions for getting wisdom.**

Special Music (Group 2): **Group 2 has learned the song, "Thy Word Have I Hid in My Heart." They are going to sing the song, then you can sing it with them. The words come from Psalm 119:11.**

Scripture (Group 3): **Group 3 has**

investigated Scriptures about Solomon and his heart. They will report their findings at this time. If time permits, read each heart piece and discuss it. Make sure you display the heart poster with all the pieces in it.

Lord's Supper: Wise people realize when they need help. We could not fight the sin in our lives by ourselves. Jesus came to give His life for us, so our sin would not condemn us forever. Have the wisdom to realize you need Him and tell Him that right now. Then thank God for sending Jesus to be our Savior.

Offering (Group 4): **This group participated in an obstacle course where they read Scriptures on wisdom and light.** Group 4 can share Scriptures they read and/or activities they did, while two other pupils collect the offering.

Devotion (Group 5): **Group 5 made a visual demonstration of a parable on wisdom. They will help me as I tell you the parable. I'm not specialized in building, but I do know a few basic facts that are very important.** If you know someone in construction who will come in to talk to the pupils, do so; then make the spiritual applications yourself.

You've all heard the song, "The Wise Man Built His House Upon a Rock." The foundation—the part you build upon—is the most important part of a house. The wise man built his house on a rock so he would have a good strong house. The point to this story is that wise people build their lives on the rock, and that rock is Jesus Christ.

But a house is not just a foundation; it's made up of other parts too. When you build your life on Jesus, the Rock, you have a strong foundation, but you need more than that. Have Group 5 members put up the pieces to show the wise man's house. **Look at this house. It is made up of windows, a door, walls, and a roof. And what does a wise person's life include?** As you mention the various parts, point to them, then read, or have pupils read, the words on the parts—Bible reading, prayer, helping others, witnessing to others, and so forth.

Do you remember what the foolish man built his house on? Yes, the sand. What do you think sand represents? (Allow for pupil ideas.) **If you build your life on sand, you're building on worldly things, things that do not last, things that do not have any strength in them. A house, or a life, built on a weak foundation will fall apart the first time there's trouble.**

So what's the point of this song? You need wisdom to decide how you want your life built. If you are wise, you will build your life on Jesus; you will choose to do what He wants you to do. Point to the words on the walls of the house. **Wise choices will strengthen you. If you build on sand and continue to make bad choices, your life is going to be weak.** Have Group 5 pupils show the visuals of the foolish man's house and read what is written on the pieces.

So what kind of house will you build? You have made a wise decision to come here today! Let's ask God for direction and help in making wise decisions.

Prayer (Group 6): **Group 6 wrote prayers based on proverbs written by Solomon.** Have volunteers read the prayers they wrote. Then close the prayer time yourself.

Closing Moments
•••••••••••••••••••••
(10-15 minutes)

God's Traffic Signs. For this activity, you'll need crayons or markers, scissors, construction paper, and samples or pictures of traffic signs. Pupils can cut out traffic sign shapes and then write mottoes about God's wisdom and direction, using the words on the signs. After pupils make their road signs, display them on a wall or door in the room.

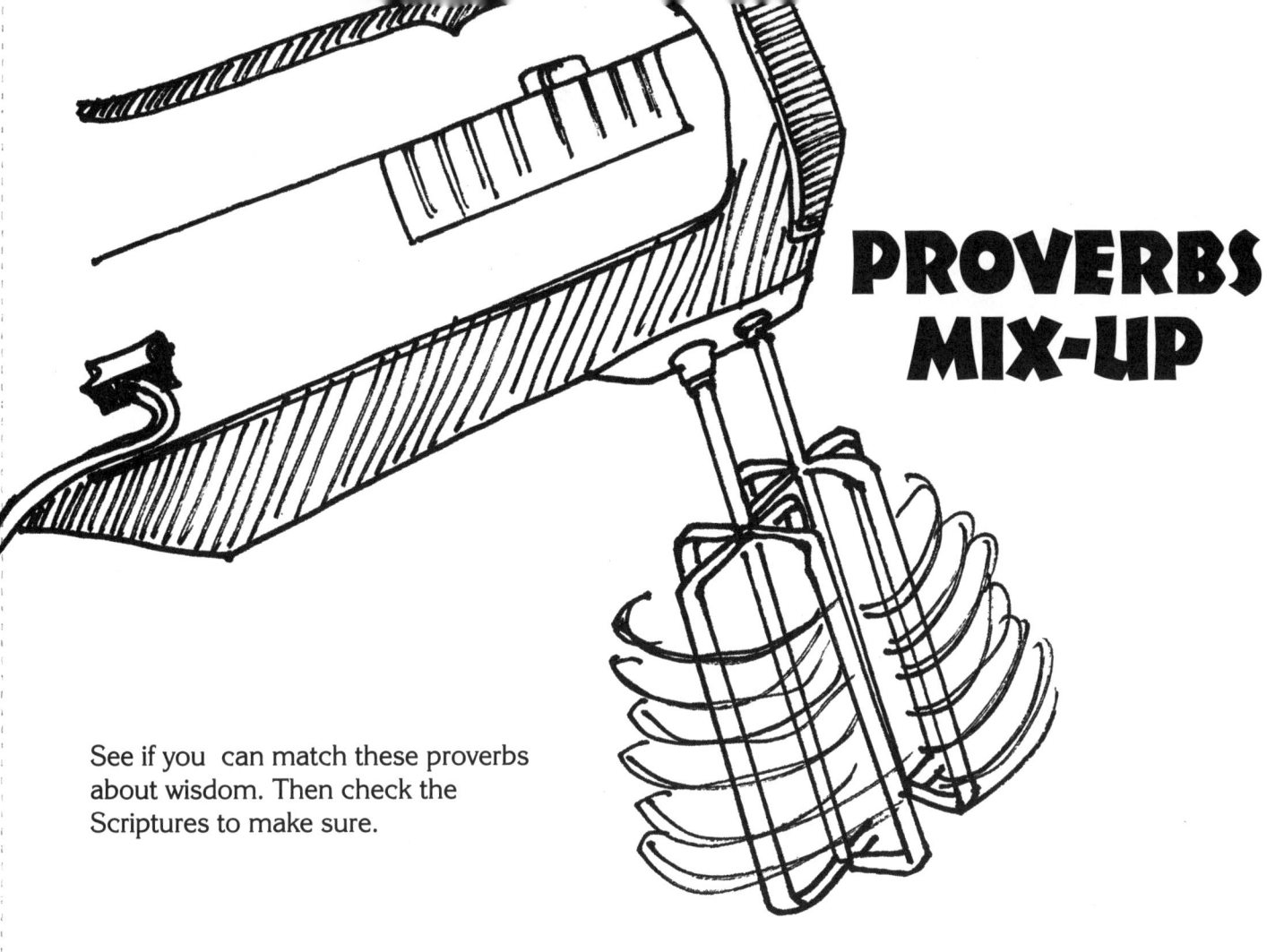

PROVERBS MIX-UP

See if you can match these proverbs about wisdom. Then check the Scriptures to make sure.

Turn your ear to wisdom,	the man who gains understanding (3:13)
Blessed is the man who finds wisdom,	but a companion of fools suffers harm (13:20)
Whoever loves discipline loves knowledge	he who cherishes understanding will find good (19:8)
He who walks with the wise grows wise,	but he who hates correction is stupid (12:1)
He who gets wisdom loves his own soul,	and apply your heart to understanding (2:2)
He who ignores teaching despises himself,	but whoever heeds correction gains understanding (15:32)
How much better to get wisdom than gold,	to choose understanding rather than silver (16:16)

Choose one of the proverbs above and write a prayer.

Dear God, since _____

_____, help me have the wisdom and strength to

choose _____

_____ Amen.

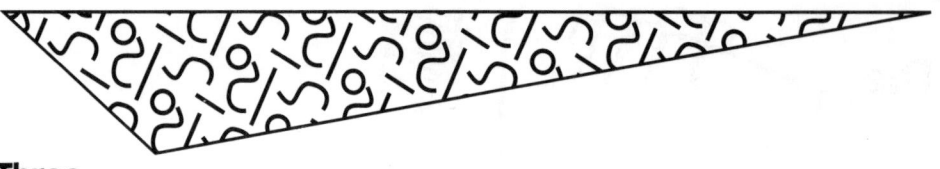

**Unit Three
Leaders Please God
Scripture Text: 2 Chronicles 2:1, 5; 3:1; 5:1, 13, 14; 6:1-3, 13; 7:1-3**

Session 13

A Respectful Heart

Worship Focus

Worship God because He deserves our honor and praise.

Transition Time

(10-15 minutes)

Prepare a set of cards for each team of five pupils. Write only the number and phrase on each card:
1. Procession with the ark (2 Chronicles 5:4-7);
2. Instruments and choir (2 Chronicles 5:12, 13);
3. Solomon's prayer (2 Chronicles 6:14-42);
4. Sacrifices (2 Chronicles 7:5);
5. People worship and give thanks (2 Chronicles 7:3).

Prepare two sets of cards with the Scripture references, to be used later. Provide poster board and markers for each team. Number each poster board from 1 to 5.

Divide pupils into teams of five. Each team lines up a set distance from their board with the five phrase cards face down on the floor in front of the board. At the signal, the first person on each team runs to the board with the marker, chooses a card from the floor, copies the phrase on the board, replaces the card face down, and gives the marker to the next person. The second person repeats what the first person did. If he or she picks up a card that has already been copied, he or she replaces it on the floor and gives the marker to the next player. The first team to complete their poster wins.

Discuss the copied list; explain that it is the order of service for the dedication of Solomon's temple. Give each team a set of the Scripture reference cards. Ask teams to find the Scriptures and match them to the phrases on their posters.

Launching the Theme

(10 minutes)

Ahead of time, ask pupils to bring in trophies, ribbons, or other awards they have received. If you or the church itself has received any awards, bring those items in too. Ask pupils to display their awards on a table where everyone can look at them. Allow time for each pupil to tell how he or she received the award.

How did it feel to receive your award? It was exciting wasn't it! It's a great feeling to receive recognition from time to time. But there is One to whom *all* praise is due: God deserves all praise and honor—all the time!. We'll discuss why today, and have the opportunity to worship God for all that He is and all that He's done for us.

Building the Theme

(30 minutes)

1. Call to Worship. Pupils in this group will design a prayer/responsive reading based on Solomon's prayer in 2 Chronicles 6:14-21. Provide several versions of the Bible, paper, and pencils.

After Solomon finished building the temple, he dedicated it to God. We're going to take a few minutes to read his prayer of dedication from several versions. Then we will write our own prayer of dedication for today's *Sharing in Worship.*

After checking the various versions, pupils will write their own prayers of dedication. Encourage pupils to think about each part of *Sharing in Worship* as they write. If you want everyone to be able to read the prayer responsively, write the words on an overhead transparency or on the chalkboard.

2. Special Music. Pupils will lead the group in singing several praise and worship songs, such as "Father, I Adore You" and "I Exalt Thee." The group will also present a song, "Holy, Holy, Holy," or "Holy, Holy" as special music. (The first song is in the hymn book; the second is in chorus books and/or some hymn books.)

Provide chorus and hymn books, pencils, paper, crayons or markers, and poster board. Tape record the special music and play it so pupils can hear all four stanzas. Practice each stanza and discuss it so pupils will understand what they're singing.

Have pupils illustrate the stanzas of the hymn, "Holy, Holy, Holy." For example:
1. Pictures of sunrise, people singing to God;
2. Pictures of people in Heaven, angels;
3. Pictures of Heaven, God;
4. Picture of everything in creation praising God.

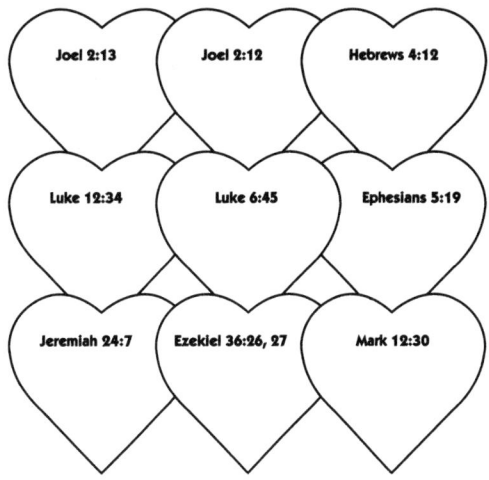

Activity Page 13A

Designate pupils to show the illustrations while the group sings all four stanzas of "Holy, Holy, Holy" during *Sharing in Worship.*

3. Scripture. For this activity, provide Bibles, pencils, and copies of Activity Page 13A. These pupils will investigate Scriptures that mention the heart. Pupils will read the Scriptures and then decide what effect their hearts have on their worship of God. You may want to assign one Scripture to each pupil to look up and then explain to the rest of the group. Tell pupils that they should be prepared to tell the whole group about their Scriptures during *Sharing in Worship.*

4. Offering. These pupils will consider which of their actions please and honor God, and prepare a gift to give to God. Provide crayons and/or markers, tape, construction paper, scissors, glue, ribbon, boxes, and wrapping paper scraps.

When you are planning to give a gift, how do you decide what to give? (Find out what the person needs or likes; fit the gift to the personality, and so forth.)

Although God does not need anything, what gift do you think He would like to receive from you? Use your imagination and creativity to design a special gift. Help the pupils to think about gifts they could give. For instance, it could be something they can make, such as a drawing, a song, or a poem. If pupils suggest something from nature, such as a beautiful flower or a sunset, remind them that those are already God's. Of course, the gift that God wants most of all is us—our love, worship, obedience, time, talents, and so forth.

Pupils should draw their ideas, and then decorate them to look like packages, or actually wrap them in boxes, paper, and ribbons. Pupils will present their ideas during the offering portion of *Sharing in Worship*.

5. Devotion. This group will participate in a skit about the dedication of the temple. You'll need pencils, copies of Activity Page 13B. Bible-times costumes and props will lend realism to the skit. Assign parts and give the group an opportunity to run through the skit a couple of times. You'll need to separate the girls and boys for the skit, since the men and women would have been in separate areas for worship. If necessary, rearrange the furniture or the room.

The skit will be presented during the Devotion.

6. Sing-a-Prayer. Pupils in this group will lead the prayer time by singing the chorus, "O Come Let Us Adore Him." Ask the pupils to write at least three new stanzas to this song. Provide Bibles, pencils, chorus books, and paper; go over the regular stanzas first.

1. O, come let us adore Him.
2. We'll give Him all the glory.
3. For He alone is worthy.

If pupils find writing new stanzas difficult, use the following words:

4. We love You and we praise You.
5. Help us to sing Your praises.
6. We honor You, O Father.

After the new stanzas have been written, they should be copied on an overhead transparency or chalkboard so the whole group can see the words. Group 6 will need to decide if they're going to sing all the stanzas as a group or have some solos. They will also need to designate which stanzas the whole group will sing together. Remind the pupils that the song should be sung quietly and reverently, since it is to be a prayer.

Sharing in Worship
(20-25 minutes)

Call to Worship (Group 1): We worship God when we honor Him and tell Him how important He is to us. Group 1 has written a responsive reading that will help us dedicate our worship service to God. Let's read together now. Group 1 gives directions on how to read responsively.

Special Music (Group 2): Many songs have been written to honor God. We'll sing some of them now. Group 2 leads the group in the worship songs they chose. Then they will sing their special song, "Holy, Holy, Holy," and show the illustrations as they sing.

Scripture (Group 3): This group investigated Scriptures about our hearts, and how they affect our worship. Ask group members to read their Scriptures and discuss them.

Lord's Supper: We honor and praise God because He is special. He can do things that no one else can do. God sent Jesus to die on the cross to take away our sins. No one else could possibly do this. Let's take time to thank God for this great gift of love.

Offering (Group 4): Group 4 discussed gifts that they can give God. Have volunteers share their "gifts" to God at this time. If there is time, ask for suggestions from the large group about gifts they can give to God.

Devotion (Group 5): **Group 5 has a skit to present to you about the dedication of the temple.** After Group 5 presents their skit, proceed with the Devotion.

When Solomon got ready to dedicate the temple to God, he took the time to praise and honor God for all He had done. Solomon mentioned at least three important aspects of God's character:

1. God keeps His promises. (Have pupils prepared to read Hebrews 10:23 and 2 Peter 1:3, 4.) **Throughout Biblical history, God always kept His Word to the Israelites. And this same God keeps His promises to us—to be with us, not to fail us, to help us. That is reason enough to honor Him.**

2. God is unique and very great. (Have a pupil read Psalm 24:1-5.) **We cannot begin to comprehend how great God is. He created everything; He is in everything; and He continues to watch over everything. We honor God, the Creator, who is involved with His creation.**

3. He answers prayer. (Have pupils read Psalms 4:3; 17:6; 145:18, 19.) **Throughout the book of Psalms, David, Solomon's father, talks over and over again about how God answered prayers. Even when you ask parents or best friends for things, they don't always give you what you want. But God always answers prayers and always comes through with the answers that are best for us. We honor God for caring for us so much that He answers prayers, not just the way we want, but in the way that is best for us.**

Prayer (Group 6): **Let's close our worship today by singing our prayers to God. Group 6 will lead us. Let's remember to sing quietly and reverently.** Group 6 will teach the new stanzas to the large group and everyone sings the prayer song, "O Come Let Us Adore Him."

Closing Moments
(10-15 minutes)

Give everyone a pencil and a copy of Activity Page 13C. Take a few moments to discuss how God answers prayers (Yes; no; later.) Then allow time for pupils to make prayer lists. Encourage pupils to pray each day and keep a record of how God answers their prayers. Ask pupils to bring their prayer pages back next week. Remind pupils that God will always answer prayers and keep His promises.

Heartfelt Gratitude

Read the Scriptures listed in the hearts below. Then write a few words about how the condition of a person's heart affects his or her relationship with God. How is the heart related to worship? How is worship influenced by the heart?

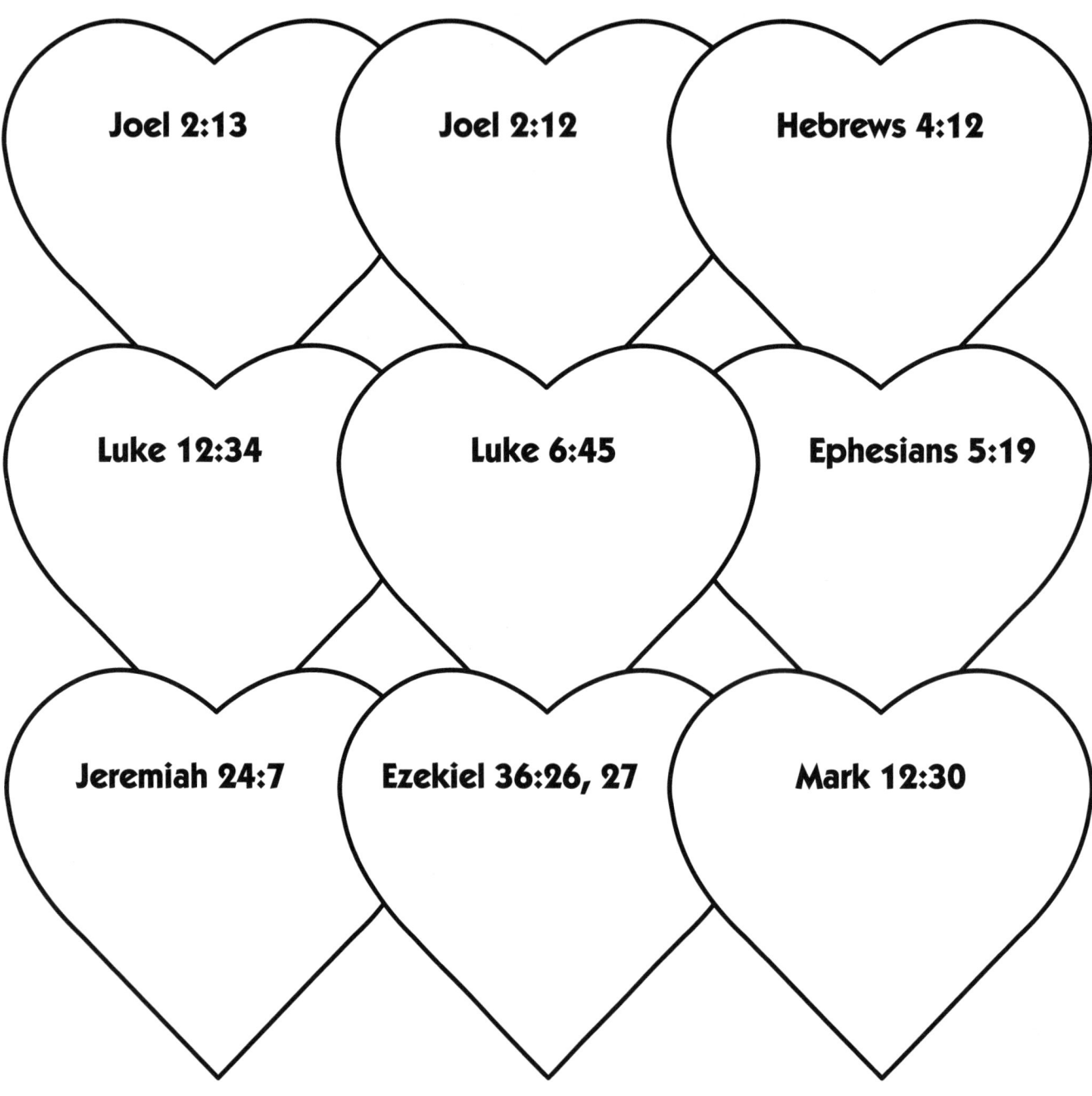

- Joel 2:13
- Joel 2:12
- Hebrews 4:12
- Luke 12:34
- Luke 6:45
- Ephesians 5:19
- Jeremiah 24:7
- Ezekiel 36:26, 27
- Mark 12:30

News Broadcast Skit

Characters: Solomon, two reporters (one man, one woman), and two people (one man, one woman); non-speaking cue card person, camera people, etc.

(Non-speaking camera people are running around as if they are setting up)

Josiah: Is everything ready? Let's roll it! . . . I'm Josiah bar Hebron.

Miriam: And I'm Miriam bar Hur, and this is the news.

Josiah: We're here today live for the dedication of the Temple. This is an exciting event!

Miriam: Yes it is exciting, and it's been quite a job—but with God's help Solomon has finished it.

Josiah: We've been watching them carry in the last furnishings for the Temple. Everything is gold and is very beautiful.

Miriam: I'm standing here with the women waiting for the proceedings to begin. Let's talk to one now. What is your name?

Rebekah: My name is Rebekah. I'm waiting for my husband. He's one of the elders helping at the dedication service today. This is truly a glorious event for the people!

Miriam: Yes, it is, and back to you, Josiah.

Josiah: I'm here talking to Uzziah. And what brings you here today?

Uzziah: My father has been helping work on the Temple. I wanted to be here for him.

Josiah: I hate to interrupt you, but it looks like they're getting ready to begin. Solomon is standing up to speak.

Solomon: (Read 2 Chronicles 6:14-21)

Miriam: Well, Josiah, Solomon highlighted some aspects of God, to whom this temple is dedicated.

Josiah: For those of you just tuning in, we've been listening to Solomon's speech for the dedication of the Temple. He's been giving God the credit and mentioned three main aspects of God:

> **1.** Solomon mentioned that God keeps His promises.
>
> **2.** Solomon mentioned how great God is, and
>
> **3.** He also stressed that God answers prayers.

Miriam: Well, God certainly has been with Solomon throughout the building of the Temple, hasn't He? Solomon really gave credit where credit is due.

Josiah: Right you are, Miriam. Our time is up, I'm afraid. We'll return to our network affiliate at this time. This is Josiah bar Hebron.

Miriam: And Miriam bar Hur signing off.

God Answers Prayer
God Keeps His Promises

Solomon mentioned again and again how good God is and how God keeps His promises. To see that for yourself, keep a prayer list for the week. Discuss together with your class prayer requests you have, and then write them here. Keep this list for the week, and then bring it back with you next week so you can see and share with others about prayers that God has answered.

PRAYER NEED	GOD'S ANSWER
_____	_____
_____	_____
_____	_____
_____	_____
_____	_____
_____	_____
_____	_____
_____	_____
_____	_____
_____	_____
_____	_____
_____	_____
_____	_____
_____	_____

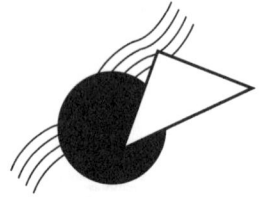
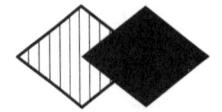

13C © 1994 by The STANDARD PUBLISHING COMPANY. Permission is granted to photocopy this page for ministry purposes only—not for resale.